To Evelyn

April 1997

THE CHURCH WITHOUT WALLS

By Thomas S. Goslin II

Los Evangelicos en la America Latina—Siglo XIX

THE CHURCH WITHOUT WALLS

Thomas S. Goslin II

Foreword by Donald McGavran

HOPE
Publishing House

P.O. Box 60008
Pasadena, CA 91106

Library of Congress
Catologing and Publication Number: 84-53037

ISBN 0-932727-00-X (pbk.)

Cover: Melissa Goslin

Thomas S. Goslin II, pastor-emeritus of the Community Church, Madrid, graduated from Yale University, did his ministerial degree at Princeton Seminary, then earned a Ph.D. from the University of Pennsylvania. Besides pastoring churches in New Jersey and Pennsylvania, he has had overseas assignments at the Union Theological Seminary, Buenos Aires and the United Evangelical Seminary, Madrid. Tom and his wife, Julia P. Cox, are in very active retirement in Wildwood, New Jersey.

For our children, who have also shared
the Community Church experience

Cay, Tom III, Bruce, Ian, Ann, and David

Table of Contents

Foreword

In this book Thomas Goslin emphasizes an essential element of the church. The church is not a building. It is a company of the redeemed. It is the body of Christ.

In the affluent society of America the church is popularly seen as a building in which church members assemble. Founding a new church means buying five acres to assure ample parking space and building an imposing ediface. Consequently, the discipling of the more than 150 million in the United States who almost never go to church and the multiplication of congregations among them have been tied to raising enough money to erect adequate buildings.

This modern American concept finds no support in the Bible. In the entire New Testament we do not find a single incidence of the Church of Jesus Christ buying one square foot of land or building any kind of a building. In New Testament times every church was a church without walls. Congregations met in homes, in upper rooms, in patios, in gardens. A few years later they met in the dead of night in underground cemeteries. Archeologists find no hint of church buildings before the year A.D. 150.

The great multiplication of Christians which went on in China since 1968 has taken place in churches without walls. The tremendous multiplication of Methodist societies in John Wesley's time took place in homes. One might almost say that every great expansion of the church has taken place by a liberated body of Christ reproducing its congregations quite freely in homes, rented halls, school buildings and other convenient meeting places. The new congregations thus founded did in many cases, as the years and decades passed, build places to meet. Church buildings are very convenient when it rains or snows. Buildings do give a sense of permanence to the congregation. They also free it from the inconveniences inherent in meeting in some home or garden. But most great growth of the church allowed each separate congregation to solve its building problem in its own way at its own time.

In Boston, Massachusetts, under the leadership of Pastor Kip McKean a church of 40 has in five years grown to a be a church of 1,400. It meets on Sunday morning in the opera house, but it also meets during the week in 150 evangelistic home Bible studies. In each of these the aim is to have attending as many nonmembers as members. Thus in the 150 house churches (evangelistic home Bible studies) some 2,000 people meet, of whom about 1,000 are interested nonmembers. The church also rents three church buildings every Wednesday night, and the members living in those sections of Boston meet there for an evening of praise, prayer and instruction.

The time has come to free world evangelization and church multiplication from the chains which attach it to the erection of commodious buildings. Let the church be seen as a company of the redeemed. Let it meet anywhere it wants. Let it build if it finds this necessary or convenient. The discipling of *panta ta ethne* (all the ethnic units of the world, Romans 16:25,) must go forward very largely indeed in churches without walls. Thomas Goslin's book will help many Christians and many pastors see the desirability—indeed the necessity—of such action.

—Donald McGavran
School of World Mission
Fuller Theological Seminary
Pasadena, California

Acknowledgements

There are a number of people to whom I would like to extend my thanks for the help they have given me with this book. First, and foremost, thanks to all of those people who were involved in the Community Church of Madrid, Spain, during the first dozen years of its life. Without them there would have been no experience to share and no book to write.

I would like to thank these friends for reading the manuscript and giving me many insightful comments during its early stages: Reverends Wm. F. Hug, Cass L. Shaw and Paul W. Stauning. These colleagues in ministry have been most helpful. Also I want to thank two former council members of the Community Church who have read and criticized the manuscript: Kathy Brue and Isabel McSpadden.

I am grateful to my son, the Rev. Ian McG. Goslin, for many helpful observations, and I would like also to give a special word of thanks to my daughter and her husband, Cay and Mark Hohmeister, for their help with getting the manuscript into its final form. And a special word of thanks to my publisher and friend, Faith Annette Sand, who has also enjoyed the Community Church experience.

I want to thank Dr. Donald McGavran for his foreword. More then 30 years ago, while on the mission field in Argentina, I first became acquainted with Dr. McGavran's thought and I hope this volume will contribute in a small way to the church growth movement.

The opinions expressed here, however, are my own and I am glad to assume responsibility for them.

Finally, a word of gratitude to my wife, Julia, who has not only encouraged me at every step of the way in writing this book but who has also shared the life of the Community Church with me over the years.

—Wildwood Crest, New Jersey
February, 1985

It was announced in the most official way that a brand new Catholic cathedral was to be built between the university and the river. No further information was given but again rumour had it that every Catholic in the diocese would have to subscribe a half-crown a week for ten years to clear the cost. As most of the population lived in Ballycastle this rumour did little to cheer them up, particularly since they had been heavily levied a short time before to prop up Maynooth College and keep it from falling into the Royal Canal. But the money was sure to be collected and the cathedral built and everyone would say publicly that it was beautiful and privately that it was a monstrous waste of money and that Christ was born in a stable.

> *—Breandan OhEithir*
> *LEAD US INTO TEMPTATION*
> *(a novel translated from Irish)*

The Community
Church of Madrid

1

Building a church without walls was something I stumbled into during a missionary term in Madrid, Spain. It turned out to be the most exciting and happiest experience of my ministry for I found myself surrounded by a congregation which chose to have no building. Rather they opted for a life-style which allowed them to concentrate their energies on supporting each other while remaining focused on the mission of the church. Gone were the budget hassles of many congregations who find themselves having to decide to repair the roof or invest in a youth program.

But to start this story at the beginning:

The Community Church of Madrid is an international, interdenominational, English-language congregation— one of over 100 English-language "union churches" found in major cities throughout the world. Many, like the American Church of Paris and the American Church of Buenos Aires, were begun in the last century.

Because of the dominance of the Roman Catholic Church, both the official and the majority church of Spain, Madrid was one of the last major cities where such a congregation was established. Spanish Protestant congregations, which began to appear in the 1860s, were illegal and always carried on their work in clandestine fashion.

Generalissimo Francisco Franco's "crusade"—closely identified with "national" Catholicism—emerged victorious at the close of the Spanish Civil War. The ranks of Protestants, decimated during the war years (1936–1939) and oppressed under Franco's dictatorship, were in more recent times generally tolerated to a certain extent as the impact of the Second Vatican Council and tourism came gradually to be felt in the late 1960s and 1970s. Franco died in 1975 and full religious liberty came finally to Spain in 1981.

In 1967 there were only three Protestant foreign-language congregations in Madrid. They survived by dint of a close identification with the embassies of their countries but maintained a ghetto-like existence.[1] With the passing of a partial and preliminary religious liberty law in 1967, it became possible to legalize existing congregations and to start new ones, under strict governmental oversight. So it was feasible to begin a union English-language congregation.

Although this had been talked about in desultory fashion for years, no action was taken until early in 1970, when an American family arrived in Madrid. The Elton Andersons had been working and living in Beirut where they had enjoyed their congregational life at the English-speaking Community Church of that city. In Madrid they were unpleasantly surprised to find no kind of union interdenominational congregation existed, so they wrote to the National Council of Churches of Christ in New York City to inquire about the possibilities of forming one. The Andersons, given my name and that of another missionary as possible contacts, got in touch with us.

I had been in Spain a little over two years as a fraternal worker with the United Presbyterian Church, assigned to teach in the United Evangelical Seminary under the auspices of the Spanish Evangelical Church which had requested my services. Prophetically enough, the original job description from the Spanish Evangelical Church listed one of my areas of service as "helping us with our ministry to foreign Protestants."

Nothing was farther from my mind than organizing an English language congregation. Nonetheless I attended a meeting with Anderson, another missionary (who was working with Cuban refugees for Church World Service), and a recently arrived couple who were also interested in an English-speaking congregation. Soon all of us and our spouses met to talk about the situation. Before the evening was over we had been prompted, we believe by the Holy Spirit, to make a serious effort to launch a union church in Madrid.

The eight of us continued to make plans. Under the new law of religious liberty, before we could even begin to meet for worship we had to submit detailed plans concerning our congregation stating what we believed, what our purpose was and where we planned to meet. We found ourselves trying to plan a church hypothetically. By laboring long and prayerfully, we emerged with a written constitution, some by-laws and a statement of faith. The government told us that while our petition to organize a congregation was being considered, we could seek police permission, week by week, to hold religious meetings.

During our planning days we made a number of decisions about the life of our still nonexistent congregation, deciding to call it "The Community Church of Madrid" and to open it to all English-speaking people, not just people from the United States. Thus we respectfully turned down the invitation of the American Embassy to hold services there initially because we did not want to become identified with any one country.

At that time we did not recognize how important our decision was never to build a building. This decision

emerged from our conviction that in a city the size of
Madrid we could easily find facilities to rent. It also
seemed foolish to try to develop loyalty to a building
program in a congregation which normally would have
more than 50 percent turnover each year. We wanted to
build the body of Christ more than we wanted to build with
bricks and mortar. This turned out to be a seminal decision
in the life of the congregation and our no-building policy is
still in effect today.

For our initial services, we were invited to use a
classroom in a little Protestant school, the *Colegio
Evangelico Juan de Valdes.* The police permit limited us to
not more than 30 adults, so our initial services were "by
invitation only" for fear of going over the permitted
number. A great deal of enthusiasm developed and almost
at once we reached the maximum.

Initially I rearranged my preaching schedule with the
Spanish Protestants so as to be free on Sunday mornings
for four to six weeks in order to get the new congregation
started. After this start-up period I was asked to continue
and eventually went on to become the founding pastor of
the congregation, serving this exciting group of believers
for twelve years (1970–1982).

The congregation was more than willing to have me
continue my teaching at the seminary where I was lecturing
in church history. But agreement was reached by the
United Presbyterian Commission on Ecumenical Mission
and Relations, the Spanish Evangelical Church and the
newly forming group whereby the Community Church
would over a period of four years assume my total support
from the denominational mission board. I began as a
volunteer with the church, and eventually became a
volunteer at the seminary with my salary paid entirely by
the church.

Within a few months of that first worship service in
March 1970, aided greatly by the Spanish Protestant Legal
Defense Commission, we received the official documents

authorizing us to organize the Community Church of Madrid (in Spanish, *Iglesia Evangelica de Habla Inglesa*). This allowed us to go public and advertise our services. Elton Anderson, the chair of the organizing committee, had business dealings with a large new hotel in Madrid. With this government permission in hand he felt we might be able to hold services there.

Soon we left the school classroom, moving to the Hotel Eurobuilding. The hotel was glad to have us because many of their guests were English-speaking and we provided a service for them. We paid them a nominal rent—which was not only a public relations gesture on the part of the hotel but also reflected the general manager's understanding of the dynamics of a group of Christians gathering to worship.

Each Sunday the hotel would assign us whatever room was available, so we did not know until we arrived just where we would gather. Over a period of seven years, the hotel found a place for us every single Lord's Day. They posted a notice in the main lobby directing people to the room chosen for the service. We met in board rooms, dining rooms, convention rooms and sometimes just in wide hallways—wherever chairs could be set up. Attendance grew from a handful to some 200 while we worshiped there. On special occasions when we knew we needed room for 300-plus, the hotel was accommodating and always managed to find someplace big enough.

Hotel employees would set up the church so chairs and a lectern were ready for us. Our hymnals (Air Force surplus, donated by the chaplains at Torrejon Air Force Base) were kept in plastic crates and along with our small electric organ on its wheeled platform were stored by the hotel between Sundays. To give us some visual help in worship, people in the congregation designed and made all kinds of banners. Quickly we learned that worship depended more on those present than on our surroundings.

Always there were the unusual and helpful experiences.

One Sunday, while we met in one-half of a very large dining room, scores of tables were being set for a banquet to be held that afternoon in the other half. The waiters worked quietly because they knew we were holding a service of divine worship, but it was a lesson for us, reminding us of the many people whose responsibilities keep them from Sunday morning worship. We were vividly aware of the privilege that was ours to be able to be at worship.

A year after the church began holding regular services it was formally organized with more than 80 charter members representing all the main line denominational families. Although the total local membership at a given time has seldom gone beyond 125, attendance invariably surpasses and often doubles the membership. Many foreigners live in a city like Madrid for a year or less, and people on the move do not want to go through ecclesiastical formalities for such brief periods of residence. It should be noted, however, that for the size of the congregation there were a large number of adult baptisms, and many adults baptized in infancy who had never before confirmed their baptismal vows did so.

After seven years, the Community Church began to outgrow the hotel, and Eurobuilding's business had picked up to the point where it lost money by renting to us at a nominal charge a room that could have easily been rented at regular commercial rates. Consequently we began to look for another place to meet. But we were not tempted to change our original decision not to build!

By this time, we had discovered many advantages to being a church without walls. We were pleased to receive an invitation from the Sacred Hearts nuns[2] who operate a large girls' school across the street from the hotel to use their worship facilities. Their large chapel, not used on Sundays although it is filled for masses several times each school day, is of contemporary architecture so all Christians can feel comfortable worshiping there.

This arrangement, which had to be approved by the bishop of the diocese, worked out very well and is still going on, seven years later. The ecumenical nature of the situation has led to positive spin-offs including joint retreats held by the nuns and members of the Community Church who are able to speak Spanish. The nuns often attend our services and have gained new understandings of Protestant Christianity. Our own people have a new appreciation of Roman Catholicism and especially those people dedicated to their educational and ministries programs.

The nuns steadfastly refuse to accept money for rent so the congregation from time to time presents them with a monetary gift requesting it be employed for the Sacred Hearts order mission schools and hospitals in the Third World. Sharing facilities across denominational lines is not new, but it is an effective way for a new church to develop an adequate place of worship without building and maintaining its own church structure.[3]

The Community Church of Madrid is distinguished by its international and interdenominational stance. Always there are members from all six continents and all races represented and usually more than 20 denominations present. The numbers include many charismatics and even Roman Catholics who have been received as associate members at their request. Beyond being a truly ecumenical congregation which has had a marked influence on hundreds of people passing through Madrid, the church without walls has served Spanish Christians as a unique model of ministry in a country noted for its abundance of beautiful, historic church buildings.

Notes

1. The three were: St. George's British Embassy Chapel, a German Protestant church, and a Southern Baptist church—the latter aimed primarily at US military personnel and dependents.
2. "Las Madres de los Sagrados Corazones."

3. In summers when the nuns go away en masse and lock the school up tight for security reasons, the congregation returns to Eurobuilding Hotel for a few Sundays.

Church Buildings
Past and Present

2

This brings me to an important point: Most Christians have a special affinity for the sanctuary where they normally worship. Though this is a book about not having church buildings, I think it is important to make clear at the outset my own love for church buildings.

Like most people I am very fond of cathedrals and have visited many of the great cathedrals of Europe and North and South America. Like most pastors I have taken a keen interest in the physical plant of the churches I have served, becoming familiar with every nook and cranny of them all.

I have many memories of clambering onto rooftops with trustees and contractors to look at slates, shingles and tarpaper and decide what needs to be done. Maintenance of facilities was always an uppermost concern of mine and I was forever calling the attention of the lay people to one or another building need, both exterior and interior.

I was also proud of our buildings. Anytime there were visitors in the manse I invariably asked, "Would you like to see the church?" Many hours I have spent showing people around sanctuary, gymnasium, Sunday school rooms, chapel, offices and kitchens, demonstrating the installations for heating, ventilation, lighting, the sound systems and the media equipment.

Then, too, like most pastors I have taken part in many a church building campaign with all that implies. I have been involved in rebuilding, renovating, making additions as well as the ultimate—building brand new facilities. Indeed, two high points in my nearly 40 years in the pastorate were leading the congregation in the first service of worship in a totally rebuilt sanctuary and participating in the ground breaking for a new Christian Education building.

Looking back on my own involvement in church building, I recall how excited and how deeply immersed I was in all the aspects: the innumerable hours of committee meetings in the planning stages, encounters with architects drawing up specifications, day-to-day and hour to hour inspections and constant supervision of the work in progress—decisions galore! Then there was the other (and extraordinarily time-consuming) aspect of church building activity: the financial campaigns.

I am glad I took part in all this because it seemed the right thing to do at the time. I never seriously questioned what we were doing. And I still enjoy visiting the church buildings in whose construction, expansion and renovation I was intimately involved. Let me make one further observation: like most pastors, I had not been prepared at seminary for that kind of responsibility and activity.

The Past

Students of church history are cognizant of the fact that during the early centuries of Christianity there were few if any church buildings. When the early church founders spoke of churches, *ekklesias,* they were referring to gathered communities of believers, not buildings. The followers of the Way gathered for worship principally, we believe, in each other's dwellings. Opposition from government developed almost instantly and believers had to meet furtively, often outdoors.

The successive great waves of persecution rolling over the church literally drove the early Christians underground. Visiting the catacombs, in the environs of Rome, we see powerful testimony to the faith of our forebears, who would not allow any emperor to stop them from gathering to worship the risen Lord, even if it meant martyrdom. What heroic times they were! How much we owe the early Christians! It still seems impossible that the handful of devoted followers of Jesus could possibly have set in motion the mighty forces that led to such rapid growth of the faith. But they did, in the power of the Holy Spirit, and we believe that the beginnings of the Christian church constitute a watershed in history (which we still divide into B.C. and A.D.).

This dynamic process over a period of some 300 years, beginning with a handful of disappointed Jews in Jerusalem, reached a climax when Christianity became the majority religion of the Mediterranean world. For the Christian, there is no more meaningful progression in all human history.

In the early church, the evangelism and mission task was carried on by communities which met in homes. They shared bread, worshiped and hosted travelers and strangers. Their firm commitment to Jesus Christ and their understanding of the church as a living organism of brothers made this loose knit collection of households a powerful missionary force.[1]

Yet this finest hour of the church happened without a single building. Imagine! No sanctuaries. No pulpits. No pews. No pipe organ. No stained glass windows. The church consisted only of people, gathered together by the power of the Holy Spirit.

Donald R. Allen, a minister interested in renewal, reminds us that the Christian community, meeting primarily in the homes of its members, survived these centuries with vigor while having no legitimate place or status. Even to join such a community put one in physical danger. Clement of Alexandria, one of the early church leaders, seems to have carried out his teaching duties in a house.[2]

With the official recognition by Constantine of Christianity as the faith of the Roman Empire early in the fourth century, the church no longer had to resort to covert activities. Christians were now able to meet in larger groups and in public buildings. The internal dynamics of the church changed.[3]

Historians are still trying to determine whether Constantine's recognition of Christianity was a blessing or something that began to change the nature of the faith to the point where we can never hope to regain the pristine character of the New Testament church. The late great church historian of the Yale Divinity School, Dr. Kenneth Scott Latourette, liked to point out how the victory won by the church through Constantine's recognition also carried with it something of defeat. This unconscious compromise came to be, in Latourette's thinking, one of the real perils for the subsequent spread of the gospel.

We must acknowledge that from the fourth century to the present, we have been involved with church buildings to such an extent that we take their presence for granted. It has become an unwritten article of faith that to carry out the Great Commission[4] we need to house our congregations in buildings especially designed and maintained for worship, Christian education and committee meetings.

In the late 20th century, however, almost without warning we have run smack into a horrendous crisis, the nature of which is just beginning to dawn upon us. This dilemma involves our centuries-long love affair with, and apparent utter dependence upon, church buildings.

These beloved buildings have become real problems. In the present economic setting we can scarcely afford to build or maintain them. Increasingly the time, money and energy we give to our buildings keep us from our principal ministry: winning adherents for Christ *and* reaching out in Christ's name to succor "the lowest, the loneliest and the lost."

Allen puts this well:

The financial bind which tightens around a congregation through its own church plant hardly needs expression, so obvious is it to most church officers. Congregations are keeping their money at home, if not for the cost of new building extensions, then for the increased cost of maintaining them. Most church plants are built through vital contributions of nominal members who understand such material needs more clearly than the intangible ones. Unfortunately, their contributions generally return to an occasional gift after the three year building debt is paid. Consequently an even greater financial burden is placed upon those committed members who must undergird the increased cost of current expenses. . . . Consider what new potential for ministry the congregations would have once their own buildings no longer strangled them with indebtedness, nor sapped the stewardship of time, with maintenance demands![5]

The Present

Because church buildings are so common, we take them for granted. No matter where you go, your attention is invariably drawn to churches—with their spires, towers and steeples. This is true in all kinds of places: city, suburb, town and country. We call to mind a stately white Congregational church on a village green in New England, a Spanish-style mission in California, a towering cathedral in Europe or a neo-Gothic edifice in New York City, prominent and unmistakable amid the skyscrapers.

When we think about the problems involved in our local congregations' buildings, most of us have to admit we face a crisis. Although the problems created by our buildings have long been with us, the petroleum crunch of 1973–1974 led to new quandaries. Many churches have had to rethink and reschedule their programming as an ever greater portion of their budget goes for electricity, gas, oil or coal. All too familiar to most congregations are the cuts imposed on programs, the consolidation of church activities on one night during the week. There has arisen the need to insulate buildings—something not dreamed of when oil cost two dollars a barrel. Thermostats have had to be turned down in the winter and up in the summer, with a corresponding decrease in the comfort of the worshipers.

Some churches in the northern tier of the United States have been forced to move their Sunday morning worship services during the winter months from their lovely sanctuaries to bare and utilitarian halls of one kind or another because their low ceilings and good insulation allow them to be warmed for a fraction of the heating costs for high ceilinged sanctuaries. Rising energy costs have also led thousands of congregations to remodel old systems or install zone heating for separately controlled areas. Many church plants built before the energy crisis had only one option: heat everything or nothing! Sometimes whole churches had to be heated just to heat the pastor's office. High energy costs are still with us and necessarily remain one of our foremost concerns.

Other serious and intriguing problems faced by churches will be discussed in the next three chapters.

Notes

1. Charles M. Olsen, *The Base Church,* Forum House, Atlanta, 1973, p. 29.

2. Donald R. Allen, *Barefoot in the Church,* John Knox Press, Richmond, VA, 1972, p. 23.

3. Olsen, *The Base Church,* p. 29.

4. Matthew 28:19-20.

5. Allen, *Barefoot in the Church,* p. 142.

Churches To Spare

3

There is a poignant sadness to the experience of worshiping with a congregation that has seen better days—where now only a small number of worshipers are left in a large building that once was crowded. This is happening more frequently these days, especially in large cities.

I will never forget one Sunday worship in a Presbyterian church in Newark, New Jersey. The church was once located in a prestigious White middle-class neighborhood, but the parish area had changed radically. Now the few White Protestants left were retired people. The rest of the present inhabitants of the area were Black or Hispanic—and poor.[1]

One's heart goes out to these people who are too often victims of racism and exploitation and we must always remember Christ's special concern for the poor. Yet few of these residents are attracted to the worship services of this church, so the building—which is often reasonably well maintained thanks to an endowment—is far too big for the present congregation (30 or 40 souls on a Sunday morning).

One has to pity the preacher who tries to lead an

effective worship service when that small number of people are spread around a 600 seat sanctuary. No one can overcome the blankness of all that empty space which gives a sense of decay and defeat, despite the fervent loyalty of the remnant that remains. The music is good, the people are friendly, there is a beautifully printed bulletin, but the congregation is obviously dwindling and dying. No evening meetings can be held except on very special occasions, and then only with suitable precautions because the neighborhood is unsafe. Usually the building has been repeatedly vandalized and so has a fortress-like appearance, common to many inner city churches.

Stories like this can be repeated ad infinitum with variations on the theme. Churches have been directly affected by the rise and fall of cities. Vast demographic changes began with the end of the American frontier toward the close of the 19th century. Population shifts, seemingly irreversible, have made thousands of churches redundant.[2] It is no secret that main line Protestants have lost the cities, at least for now, and it is tragic that money and energy have been poured into maintaining these vast old structures that are totally unsuited for contemporary urban ministry. It is sad to see beautiful Gothic and colonial church edifices falling into ruins, being torn down or used for restaurants, night clubs, warehouses—uses far from the minds of the Christians whose toil, tears, joy and devotion went into building them.

Nor is selling the building to another congregation the answer. The new congregation often has trouble paying even the greatly reduced price. Often the sanctuary, built for austere and cerebral main line Protestant worship, does not easily lend itself to the spontaneous, less structured liturgies of the new congregation. One must admire the fervent enthusiasm and dedication of these congregations and admit they have much to teach us about taking Christianity seriously. But when they acquire old buildings, the same maintenance problems are there, only worse: the roof is older, the plumbing and wiring are more antiquated, the organ is obsolescent, the carpet is worn— and sometimes the new owners are ultimately forced to abandon the building, too.

Any devoted Christian will have misgivings when contemplating the huge amount of time, energy and money thrown into the unequal struggle to keep a church plant going after a change in the neighborhood. Our church building experience has taught us to build for the centuries, but our neighborhoods sometimes last for as little as a generation.

What happens to the congregation that sells and runs? Usually they head for a new location a good distance away, in the heart of a safe or growing area, and there duplicate the old facilities. Again this involves enormous expenditures of time, energy and money. The risk of collapse, however, has not been overcome—it has only been postponed until new changes occur.

As Americans we have a sad history of building cities, then gradually abandoning them to their fate, and to the poor. We move farther away and start a new urban sprawl. And churches have thus far been unable to invent a strategy to circumvent this vicious cycle. Wallace Stegner, the essayist, writes:

We have been fruitful and multiplied; we have spread like ringworm from sea to sea and from the 49th parallel to the Rio Grande; but in doing so we have plundered our living space. If we have loved the land that fate gave us, and most of us did, we went on destroying it even while we loved it, until now we can point to many places we once pointed to in pride, and say with an appalled sense of complicity and guilt, "Look what we've done."
3

The problem of excess churches affects every major urban area in the United States. Neither urban renewal nor gentrification (upgrading of decaying areas) seems destined to overcome this problem, except in a limited fashion.

Even when a congregation survives, there are often other problems. Perhaps the new highway that needs to be built leaves a church all of a sudden condemned so the road can go through. Or worse, the church might be spared, only to remain in splendid isolation cut off from its natural parish by ribbons of concrete. Driving through Newark, New Jersey on the Garden State Parkway, one passes many churches hemmed off in this fashion.

Occasionally the problems are entirely different. Witness the churches in urban areas such as on Wall Street in New York, where the land becomes so valuable for commercial use that enormous sums of money are offered to a church to relocate. New tensions come to these congregations. Should they take the munificent sum and move, or stay despite all offers? A congregation can easily be thrown into crisis by the fantastically large offers of money made for all or even part of its property. Not many of us as Christians are spiritually prepared for such temptation. But as long as the church holds real estate, this can happen.

One seemingly viable solution is that of St. Peter's Lutheran Church in New York City, which sold its church site at 55th and Lexington to permit construction of the Citicorp Center Development, which contains a newer, smaller church. This is a praiseworthy experiment. There are cases like this elsewhere. The World Council of Churches has a program that helps churches develop their land for commercial use. Usually the existing church is torn down and a new building is erected. The congregation retains the right to use one or two floors and benefits from renting the additional stories.

City churches are not alone, of course, in their problems. Monthly utility bills must be paid whether you are a city, suburban, town or country congregation. Many rural churches are abandoned when people move to larger centers of population. As the number of Americans owning farms decreases, the problem of excess rural churches will become more serious.

When we think about redundant churches, we sense that

we have long been entranced by our buildings. The late Thomas Merton, Roman Catholic monk and author of many books, talked about the concept of sacred space as it has formed the religious consciousness of the West. This concept is intimately related to sacred architecture. According to Merton, Christian architecture took over the domed aula or the vast basilica, and the fantastic exploitation of space and light in the Gothic cathedral made a symbolic representation of the whole cosmos. He went on to say:

The cathedral is a "world" created by walls on which every kind of being is represented, by windows through which the light of heaven pours in on the people of God, by a spiritual and hidden sanctuary in which the sacred mysteries are represented. Here the conceptions of transcendence and immanence are both present.[4]

Merton believes that this was an extremely sophisticated and profound theological vision that we have lost, and he said that it was no longer possible to fit this kind of church into the "space" of our cities and of our world. This Roman Catholic monk wanted us to become aware of the fact that our new consciousness of space no longer admitted the traditional religious imagery by which we represent to ourselves our encounter with God. He asserted that this traditional imagery was never essential to Christianity: "We must recover the New Testament awareness that our God does not need a temple (Acts 7:47-53) or even a cathedral. The New Testament teaches the fact that God has an indestructible temple, which is the person (I Corinthians 3:17)."[5]

Notes

1. In May 1983 Newark had the highest percentage of people below the poverty line of any American city over 100,000 population: 32%.

2. The word "redundant" is officially used, for example, in the Church of England's "Commission on Redundant Churches."

3. Wallace Stegner, *One Way to Spell Man,* Doubleday & Co., New York, 1982, p. 163.

    4. Thomas Merton, *Conjectures of a Guilty Bystander,* Doubleday
& Co., Garden City, New York, 1966, pp. 273-274.
    5. Ibid.

Church Buildings
As Problems

4

Rev. John Harrington, rector of the Anglican parish in Doddington, England, has banned all fund raising events because he contends his church is getting a reputation as a professional beggar. He says:

When you meet people in the pub or village and they make jibes about being badgered for money then the time has come to stop. I've become a standing joke. When people see me coming they say: "Here he is again . . . how much does he want this time?"

Harrington believes that repeated requests for money are driving people away from the church. "It seems that our only interest in them is what they will give us." This rector has cancelled a garden fete and flower festival, among other events, destined to raise 30,000 pounds for church repairs, remarking that it seemed a selfish luxury to ask for that much money for a church roof which is used for a few hours a week "when one-third of the world hasn't got a roof over its head at all." [1]

A recent study of 50 congregations indicates that more church dollars are being spent for utilities and correspondingly fewer for benevolences and pastoral services. This means that there is less money for projects beyond the local congregation, and smaller amounts sent to mission boards.[2]

According to Dr. Martin E. Carlson, former director of administration and finance for the Lutheran Church in America, the basic costs of operation take a larger percentage of the church budget than they did a decade ago. A study by the Hartford Seminary Foundation indicates that the middle-sized church, with a membership ranging from 400 to 800, has the most difficulty keeping up with inflation.[3]

It may be that both small and large churches benefit from the economy of scale: the larger ones can support building and program, the smaller ones never had a full program anyway, while the middle-sized church needs both program and building but does not have money for both. Despite this and many similar observations, this study reports that most leaders of congregations having financial problems are more optimistic than the condition of their churches warrants.[4]

To see how some congregations are affected by conditions noted in these studies, let us study Philadelphia, Pennsylvania, examining both a group of congregations and then some individual congregations.

A Group of Congregations

The strip of Chester Avenue from 55th to 58th streets in Philadelphia contains seven churches. The two oldest churches in this three block area are the Most Blessed Sacrament (Roman Catholic) and the Westminster United Presbyterian. The exterior of each covers an entire city block, but neither comes close to filling its interior with worshipers. The five other churches are much newer to the neighborhood and are small enough that combined, they could fit inside the sanctuary at Most Blessed Sacrament, whose twin cupolas tower over the surroundings.

Since the mid '60s, the number of families in Most Blessed Sacrament has plunged from about 7,000 to 600. The congregation was all White but is now predominantly Black. In the last three years the church has lost 200 families. This surely reflects the mobility of our times in America, where one family in four moves every year. One writer notes: "Change becomes the basic building block of life." [5]

A member of the parish, Delia Sweet, reflects, "It's a shame, really. We used to be in the sacristy, inside the railings and everywhere, alongside the aisles, and if someone like a missionary came you'd have to go an hour early." Sweet has been a member for 48 of her 70 years.

What is it like there today? A reporter writes:

Up in the choir of the immense Southwest Philadelphia church, so distant from the altar that only the pastor's rich green vestments made him discernible, a Sunday morning swelter was rising. Small collections and $55,000 a year utility bills had shut down the air-conditioning. The eight choir members, sweat soaking through their clothes, offered a listless rendition of "Morning Has Broken" as 150 parishioners, many of them elderly, shuffled down aisles longer than a basketball court. They scattered among the 1,200 seats, which were usually filled a dozen years ago when everybody in the neighborhood was Irish.[6]

Most Blessed Sacrament during its height in the 1960s had the largest parochial school enrollment in the nation, but the enrollment dropped from 3,400 to 260 in 1981-1932. Buildings that were once filled with school children now are closed. "We have, for all practical purposes, a couple of mausoleums—empty buildings—to keep up," said the rector, Father H. Thornton Kelly.

At Westminster Presbyterian, the other ancient, large church in the neighborhood, the pastor, Rev. John Hollingsworth, reported that while many of his church members continued to attend the Chester Avenue church after they moved to the suburbs, their interest in the church's neighborhood declined. One of the buildings in the complex, which occupies an entire block, has had to be closed.

When we look at the other five churches in this section of Chester Avenue, we find they are smaller, interdenominational churches that began in living rooms and basements and have now moved to storefronts. To put it another way, the big churches in this area have been closing buildings and the smaller ones have been buying buildings, but in no case is there any attempt to duplicate the splendors of Most Blessed Sacrament and Westminster United Presbyterian. The new churches have sprung up, not simply because a distressed area needed evangelizing, but also because it offered relatively cheap real estate, a place to rise from the ashes.[7]

Individual Congregations

Two other congregations in the Philadelphia area help shed light on our subject. The first is the Tabernacle Presbyterian Church. Built over a century ago at the corner of 37th and Walnut, it is a large Gothic-style stone edifice with a tower on the corner. Nearly everything around it has changed, and now it may be the church's turn to change.

The Tabernacle people are realizing they no longer can afford to keep the building going, and maintenance has been delayed for years. One of the most apparent possibilities would be to exploit the site for commercial development and to tear down all (or at least a part) of the historic structure. An awareness has dawned that even if money were not a problem, the 100-year-old plant does not meet the present needs of the congregation.

Tabernacle, which is liberal in its social attitudes, has many people who have ties to the University of Pennsylvania or Drexel University and are therefore transient. Turnover in this congregation is high. The present membership of about a hundred is obviously much smaller than the membership for which the church was built.

Ten years ago Tabernacle, like other churches, was spending 18 to 20 percent of its income for heating and utility bills, but now this can be 60 to 70 percent. In 1981 the church spent $80,000, of which $25,000 went into the upkeep and expenses of the building. The giving of the congregation amounted to only a little more than $40,000.

The deficit was covered by rentals and aid from the Presbytery of Philadelphia. In 1981 Tabernacle earned $20,000 by renting space in its church and parish house to various groups, but one of its chief tenants, a Korean congregation, has announced that it is leaving. In an endeavor to keep expenses down, the lovely sanctuary is not used between All Saints Day in November and Palm Sunday.

This surely brings before the Tabernacle people a crucial question: should they continue to spend money on a building they love, or focus on their mission to people? Compounding the problem is the fact that Tabernacle Church is a historic building and an important work of architecture, designed by Theophilus Parsons Chandler, first dean of architecture at the University of Pennsylvania.

The eventual solution may well be not for the congregation to sell, but to make arrangements to stay as part of a larger development. It could follow the example of St. Peter's Church in New York City,[8] or it could imitate St. Bartholomew's Episcopal Church on Park Avenue at 50th Street in New York which has talked about tearing down its parish house to make way for a high-rise office building.

The Tabernacle people also have discussed asking the University of Pennsylvania to increase its use of their buildings, or even to take them over. The congregation wants to stay where it is and the Presbytery of Philadelphia, the ultimate owner, wants to maintain its presence on the university campus. Every conceivable possibility has been discussed over the years, including building apartments for senior citizens or converting the sanctuary into a restaurant.

The continuous dilemma is well expressed in the words of a trustee of the congregation, William Lovett:

If some alternative that involved getting rid of the building looked really good, I might be willing to consider it. The church is not the building. If and when we really examine whether we stay here or not, it will be very difficult for many people.

Another member, who was involved in a similar process in Rochester, New York, says:

The building itself becomes symbolic of a considerable investment of your life. In Rochester, I realized that the church building had great meaning for me, the history of the buildings had great meaning for me, and the loss of them left me disoriented because they symbolized a community of which I felt myself to be a part.[9]

The second Philadelphia-area church to look at is the Madison Street Methodist Church in Chester which once boasted 2,000 members and a crowded Sunday school. Today there are scarcely 50 people present on Sundays, the youngest member is 70 and there is no longer a Sunday school. It is more common for the pastor to preside at funerals than to perform weddings. Madison Street's members have scattered throughout Delaware County over the years.

Their church is now following them. The congregation has announced plans to merge with Christ United Methodist Church on Dutton Mill Road in Middletown Township. Christ Church moved out of the city 18 years ago! Many other churches have moved out in the meantime, as a consequence of demographic and economic changes in Chester in the last 40 years.

In 1940, there were 66,000 residents—52,000 White and 14,000 nonwhite. The 1980 census reflected a huge change: 46,000 population—19,000 Whites and 27,000 nonwhites. Now unemployment is high and a large portion of the inhabitants live below the poverty level. As White residents have left the city, so have many of their congregations. Often the abandoned sanctuaries have been sold to members of the predominantly Black community that remains.

The pastor at Madison Street United Methodist, Rev. James R. Hoover, says, "We are trying to do what will bring life into the church in the future." The building will be sold to Little Refuge Apostolic Church of Our Lord Jesus Christ, a predominantly Black church that started in a living room 34 years ago. This congregation expects to grow, now that it has larger facilities.

One of Madison Street's members said, "It just doesn't seem possible that this could happen. It's a shame. There are a lot of memories." [10]

In his satiric column in *The Christian Century,* Martin E. Marty writes, "When natural gas deregulation comes in the next few years, says my friend, this example of capitalist free enterprise will lead to the closing of one-third of the inner-city churches of my city or your city. No little congregation can keep the fires going or the walls warm."

Marty continues,

Yet a problem will remain. What do we do with all the empty hulks that will dot the cityscape? They have already been, in sequence, fashionable WASP churches, followed by Mogen Davided synagogues, Black temples and Hispanic churches. Now only four cold walls, sagging roofs and overlays of symbols remain. I've shuffled around inside some of these derelict buildings with church extension executives or morose representatives of bishops. "Yes, we'd love to tear 'em all down, if we could. But have you ever gotten an estimate on what it takes to destroy a building?" I have not, but one does not need much skill to estimate what estimates would look like.[11]

Marty suggests dynamite, and winds up with the ironic suggestion that film companies might be interested for pictures with the setting of any Central American nation. He says, "Blow it up, film it, market it, and save the church some money."

It would certainly save money. For instance, the Tioga Presbyterian Church in Philadelphia is spending $75,000 to demolish its sanctuary and manse.[12]

Notes

1. *Daily Telegraph*, August 1, 1981.

2. *Yearbook of American and Canadian Churches*, 1981, quoted in *Mission Memo*, July-August 1981, an occasional publication of the UPCUSA.

3. The *Miami Herald*, November 27, 1980, p. 5-B.

4. *News Notes*, West Jersey Presbytery, September 1980.

5. Olsen, *The Base Church*, p. 2.

6. *Philadelphia Inquirer*, August 1, 1982, p. 3-A.

7. Hank Klibanoff, "Faith, Hope and a Sense of Place," *Philadelphia Inquirer*, August 1, 1983, pages 1-B and 6-B.

8. See Chapter 2.

9. Thomas Hine, "Congregations That Can't Afford Their Churches Look for a Way Out," *Philadelphia Inquirer*, July 26, 1982, pages 1-D and 7-D, passim.

10. Suzanne Gordon, "Chester Church Joins Exodus to Suburbia," *Philadelphia Inquirer*, July 3, 1983, pages 1-B and 4-B, passim.

11. *The Christian Century*, November 17, 1983, p. 1183.

12. *Minutes* of Philadelphia Presbytery, July 26, 1983, p. 3.

Stalled New Church Development

5

"Make your congregations exciting centers for mission." So spoke the Rev. David W. Preus, general president of the American Lutheran Church, to the Presbyterian General Assembly meeting in Phoenix, Arizona in June 1984. "People don't want to belong to moribund organizations," he said. "The excitement comes in the outreach."

The distinguished Lutheran did remind his hearers, however, that many Lutheran and Presbyterian congregations "are more maintenance-minded than mission-minded." [1]

That is the basic question: Is our congregation more maintenance-minded or more mission-minded? Our buildings inevitably impel us to be maintenance-minded. Many congregations spend huge amounts of money on the upkeep of buildings, and only paltry sums for missions.

The church growth movement inspired by Dr. Donald McGavran and his associates at Fuller Seminary in California is germane to this theme. The now vast church growth literature has brought home the need to establish new congregations. This is the only way we can fulfill the biblical mandate: "to . . . teach . . . make disciples."

There is a direct relationship between church multiplication and membership growth. Research has shown that a central activity in the growth process is the planting of new churches. These new congregations provide the growing edge for a denomination, and those denominations which grow most rapidly are usually the ones that put great emphasis on church multiplication.

New church development, however, has stalled in the main line denominations in the United States. This is not because of a lack of evangelistic zeal; neither is it because of a lack of clergy willing and able to undertake new church development. Nor is it a lack of geographical areas that need new churches. There are still boom areas— Florida, Texas, Arizona, California—where denominations need to keep pressing new church development.

Why, then, has this development slowed down so much? Principally because the cost of building has exceeded the reach of the typical newly formed congregation. The mission help once available from denominational headquarters is, in most cases, no longer there.

At the meeting of the General Assembly of the United Presbyterian Church in 1981, commissioners were told that 34 new congregations had been launched during the previous year as part of a five-year plan to begin more than 150 new churches. But the commissioners agreed with a committee recommendation that a multimillion-dollar program for the construction of new church buildings could not be undertaken in 1985 as planned.[2]

What about the financial responsibility of the members of new congregations? One estimate is that at least 300 pledging units, averaging six to seven dollars a week, are needed just to be able to go forward with a structure. There are many areas where it is not possible to bring that many people together in a relatively short time so as to meet this challenge. Also, people hesitate to become involved in a new congregation that obviously is going to need massive financial support from its members over a long period of time just to achieve the minimum in a building program.

There is a new church development called Robyn's Roost, on the growing edge of a major metropolitan area, that has been helped by mission development funds from headquarters. The organizing pastor, three years on the field, is both delighted and frightened. He reports "marvelous good feelings about the closeness of the people who have chartered our new church." At the same time he says he has nightmares about the nearly half-million-dollar debt they will assume when their projected first unit is completed.[3]

Most pastors and lay leaders have come up against the wariness of new people who seem to be looking for a church where there is abundant parking, a building already paid for, and no immediate prospects of a new building fund.

The first question asked me by a new visitor at the Community Church of Madrid one Sunday morning was whether we were planning to build a building. When I said, "No," this newcomer was visibly relieved and replied, "Good. In the last five places I've lived, I've had to support building programs and I don't want to have to do it again."

After all, the cost of maintenance and utilities in a normal parish is already very high, without the added burden of construction costs and debt amortization. The amount of money the denomination can put into new church development is crucial. Denominations provide considerable assistance with outright grants, low interest loans, and even "silent" (deferred interest) loans. But as construction costs increase, as interest rates remain high, the amount of money that would have sufficed for 25 congregations a few years ago will hardly do for five today.

This makes for hard choices in denominational headquarters. It also simply means that fewer and fewer new church development projects can be adequately funded by denominational home mission boards. There are national drives by the denominations from time to time that include in their goals large sums of money for new church development. But the need for new churches has grown beyond the financial resources of both the developing congregations and the denominational treasuries.

Traditional patterns of church growth, which lead to the construction of elaborate sanctuaries, also make difficult any genuine participation by the poor and needy. To neglect the oppressed is a clear violation of scriptural standards of justice.

There is another crucial aspect to the whole matter. Is it wise to help a new congregation acquire facilities for worship and Christian education when it is a foregone conclusion that the payment of the mortgages and the continuing charges for maintenance and the use of those buildings will demand a major portion of that congregation's time, money and effort for the foreseeable future?

I strongly question the wisdom of this, even though such decisions are made so many hundreds of times in any given year that they seem beyond question. Indeed such choices become almost automatic. And here is the crux of the issue that has called forth this book.

It has been truly said that the physical facilities a congregation acquires determine the shape of its ministry. It is inevitable that when you have a building you feel obligated to use it and to center your entire program in it. The Christian education facilities can be used weekdays by nursery schools, Boy Scouts and Girl Scouts, Alcoholics Anonymous, exercise classes, basketball leagues and the like. But the sanctuary is seldom used except on Sunday mornings, even in the case of a congregation with an attendance that requires duplicate services.[4]

Most main line groups have long since given up weeknight services except for special occasions. The advent of television following World War II dealt a death blow to the evening service in many Protestant congregations. At least that is when my evening service expired.

There is always the occasional wedding, concert and presbytery-district-classis-diocesan meeting, but the sanctuary stands there unused for days and nights on end. In the present needy world, is this truly the way the Lord of life would have us employ our resources? To move toward the Kingdom, do we really have to keep on building sanctuaries, with heat, light, air-conditioning, stained glass windows, carpets, organs, cushioned pews and various ecclesiastical oddments? Once you get started, it is hard to stop.

We have been told that "we gather to scatter" and that "the service (to the world) begins when the benediction is pronounced." But is this really true? Our chief emphasis seems to be on getting the people to come to the building: for worship, for meals, for recreation, for self-improvement, for whatever. It makes me uneasy that we have that building. It should make us all uneasy.

We don't talk or even think much anymore about the Last Assize or Final Judgment (Matthew 25). Think how you would explain your church building when you were making your final accounting to the Lord. What would he reply to your explanations as to why you had to have a building with all the amenities even though you used it only on Sunday mornings? Would you say, "Everybody else has one"? Would you say, "We couldn't think of anything else to do"? Would you say, "After all, it is dedicated to the Father's honor and glory"? I hesitate to think of some of the Lord's responses to such logic.

Today I feel myself privileged to have worked with at least one congregation, this vibrant group in Madrid (and there are others), which decided to say, "We choose not to build a sanctuary," and then went on to develop an alternative style of congregational life. Little did we know how influential our decision not to have a building of our own would become regarding the way we grew and developed. Obviously, the decision *not* to have a building has just as much impact on a congregation as the prevalent decision to *have* a building, but the consequences are quite different.

Notes

1. Allen Kratz, *General Assembly Daily News,* June 7, 1984, p. 8.
2. *A.D.* magazine, June-July 1981, p. 41.
3. Ibid, p. 26.
4. Roman Catholics and Episcopalians, who use their sanctuaries weekdays as well as Sundays, are notable exceptions. Even with these churches, however, it should be noted that weekday attendance at worship services tends to be meager.

The House
Church Movement

6

Christians everywhere have been thrilled to learn of the resurgence of the church in the People's Republic of China. Over the years small Christian communities, meeting in homes, have kept the faith alive during one of the most radical upheavals in human history. These groups met in homes or other private places when it was not possible for them to meet publicly as a church.

One such community has been meeting since 1969: eight Christian families living in a five-house compound opening up to an inner court. They meet in one of the houses, sitting in the house itself, the covered porch and the open court. In the winter, they squeeze all the elderly people inside and the young people pack themselves into the porch. Since early 1980 when the government announced that the policy of religious freedom guaranteed by the constitution would be put into practice, they have had three services each Sunday. As a result, many people have been coming to worship.

This house church is only one of a network of some 400 in the southeast provinces alone. A member reports, "We are still worshiping in homes. . . . The only church building

left standing has no roof and it is some six kilometers
away. I don't see the possibility of erecting a new church.
There are no laws, no regulations, no permission." [1]

Another observer of the China scene writes:

The revival of Christian worship is taking place in virtually every
province. The survival of the faith for many years without public
worship and clergy leadership is attributable to neighborhood
and village "house meetings" and family devotions and nurture.
It is assumed that persons from these house meetings form the
core membership. [2]

The strength of the house church movement in China has
alarmed the government. Reports of renewed persecution
are beginning to filter out. The victims are leaders of the
house churches. Many have been arrested and while some
have been released others are still being held. [3]

The house church movement, not only in China but in
many countries, is a valid approach to starting a new
congregation. Let us briefly examine the development of
this movement in the United States since it touches upon
and informs our basic theme. [4]

In recent years in America there has been
experimentation with different congregational life-styles.
It is nothing new to find that many people are dissatisfied
with congregational forms and practices that seem
concerned more with self-preservation than with service,
more with budgets and buildings than with human needs
and relationships.

One writer points to this phenomenon, saying: "Persons
who describe themselves as 'critical of, but committed to
Christ's church, dedicated to exploring and developing
faith-filled life-styles having integrity, meaning and a
contagion that is evident and embracing' . . . have tried
many new ways of congregational life." [5]

Many of these experiments have led to what is being
called house churches—a term which can mean many
things. Rev. Charles M. Olsen, director of Project Base

Church in Atlanta, Georgia, 1973–1975, gives the definition of house church as a group

of eight to 20 people who meet in an informal setting, usually in a home or small, comfortable room. By "church" I mean that this group has a self-consciousness that the group is a church, that it is intentional about its worship, caring and ministry . . . and that it sees itself as part of the larger church, whether formally attached to a denominational parish or congregation or informally relating to the larger Christian community through an ecumenical entity or network of other house churches.[6]

There are many people gathering in groups that are small enough for informal and intimate relationships, Olsen adds. "They are not uniform or easily controlled," he continues. "Some are liturgically centered, some are intergenerational, some are communal, some are mission-action centered, some are charismatic, some exist for support and personal growth, some have roots in the human potential movement, but they have enough common features to be identified as a movement." [7]

House church enthusiasts say that in church history the small group has normally accompanied renewal movements. The Wesleyan class meetings attested to this. Martin Luther wanted house groups to come together "to pray, to read, to baptize, to receive the Sacrament, and to do other Christian works." [8]

Olsen states, however, that "by the mid '70s the house church as an alternative structure had fallen off dramatically" and that by the end of Project Base Church in 1975 most of the attention had turned to renewed hope for traditional congregations.[9]

The late Dr. Paul Calvin Payne, general secretary of the Presbyterian Board of Christian Education in the '40s and '50s, was fond of saying "if it doesn't happen in the local church, it doesn't happen."

There are advantages and problems in the house church movement. Proponents say that they experience "the event

of community," of building and experiencing Christian
fellowship, of knowing "community" as a means of grace,
of experiencing theologically charged words such as love,
trust, grace, affirmation and healing in a fresh way. "The
church is event. Something happens. Ministry takes place
wherever two or three are gathered." [10]

Another writer on this theme, A. Wayne Benson, states
that although it was not anticipated, the house church's
life-style proved to appeal to people who were dissatisfied
with the traditional church's life-style. People who have
dropped out of church or have not previously associated
with it are now involved in the life and work of the church,
a fact that underscores the need for such a life-style in the
broad spectrum of the church's life. It also merits attention
as a means of reaching out to people who are often
untouched or unresponsive to traditional congregations. [11]

It is worthwhile to look at the experiences of some of
these house churches as new expressions of congregational
life because there often has developed a sense that all the
members in the congregation are in ministry. The World
Council of Churches' Assembly in New Delhi (1961)
reflected this sense by requesting a study on the missionary
structure of the local congregation. [12]

At one point in the house church movement, the United
Presbyterian Church promoted what were known as issue-
centered congregations. An attempt was made to
distinguish this particular type of congregation from the
more traditionally styled churches. As the history of each
of the groups established within that newer framework
unfolded, it became ever clearer that few people were
attracted to these congregations because of their issue
focus. The attraction was not in the issue (race, welfare,
public education, and so forth) but in the style of the
congregation. These groups began to be called style-
centered rather than issue-centered.

Few if any of the style-centered congregations achieved
a size beyond 30 to 40 adult members. Many families

retained membership in the congregations from which they came and most were heavily involved in the program and operation of their former congregation. Also, hopes that the specially focused, buildingless congregations would attract a great number of younger people were not realized. The age of people involved as members in these congregations was generally 40 to 55.

The most severe problem of the house church, however, has been the financial one. Denominational headquarters have not been in a position to add to the monies of the budgets of these congregations to make up for the deficits resulting from fewer members and donations than anticipated. National monies, even when the original plan was for more than a three-year support span, have not been enough to carry the congregations' budgets when added to the income from the congregations. Several congregations have had to make premature decisions about their life together because they could not provide adequate funds to keep an organizing pastor on the field.[13]

The combination of small numbers and inadequate financing has blocked the proliferation of these churches in the United States. There are limited growth possibilities in one intimate group. Isolation is encouraged because no structure exists for relationships with other groups.[14]

Anne Lee Kreml, a new church development specialist, says that "the close, intimate community which develops in the house church is so foreign to our usual experience that we tend to hand it on to the exclusion of other people. It is very easy for the house church to develop into an experience of idolatry."[15]

Olsen says: "Without support, connection and accountability, [this kind of church] is doomed to a short life. I insist that the basic communities must be connectional."[16]

The late Gordon Skadra, a Presbyterian mission executive, voiced his concern that we had become too "scientific" in our endeavors to study new church development:

We have dissected the parish church concept quite heavily over the past 30 years. We need to begin to appreciate the congregation as a whole thrust of the Holy Spirit. We need to be able to affirm the life and meaning of the congregation as the first line of the church's witness and mission.[17]

Notes

1. Raymond Fung, *Households of God on China's Soil,* World Council of Churches, Geneva, 1982.

2. Dr. Donald MacInnis, *The Christian Century,* April 1, 1981.

3. Cited in "A Church in Crisis Weeps and Prays," *Time,* September 17, 1984.

4. There is a brief history of house churches in Donald K. Allen, *Barefoot in the Church,* John Knox Press, Richmond, VA, 1972, pp. 22–36.

5. *Alternate Life-styles, An Exploration,* a study paper on small groups and house churches in the Presbytery of the Palisades, prepared by the Johnsons, Millers and Ropers, August 1973, privately printed.

6. Charles M. Olsen, "Ministry Where Two or Three Are Gathering," paper read to the annual meeting of the Fellowship of Christian Ministries, Chicago, IL, August 31, 1974.

7. Ibid, p. 1.

8. *Preface, The German Mass and Order of Service,* quoted in Olson, *The House Church Revisited,* privately printed, 1981, p. 2.

9. Ibid, p. 6.

10. Olsen, op. cit., p. 4.

11. A. Wayne Benson, *An Alternative Congregational Life-style,* unpublished doctoral dissertation, San Francisco Seminary, June 1974, p. 9.

12. See *The Quest for Structure of Missionary Congregations,* World Council of Churches Department of Studies in Evangelism, Geneva, 1965.

13. Gordon Skadra, "Does Anybody Really Know What Time It Is?" paper read at the Consultation on New Congregations for Growing Suburban Areas, Houston, TX, January 29–31, 1974.

14. Olsen, *The Base Church,* pp. 73–78.

15. Anne Lee Kreml, "Creating Community Through the House Church," paper prepared for the Consultation on New Congregations for Growing Suburban Areas.

16. Olsen, *The Base Church,* p. 19.
17. Skadra, "Does Anybody Really Know What Time It Is?"

Starting A
Buildingless Church

7

Starting churches in homes is exciting! When we become discouraged about our slow progress in church planting, especially in historic denominations in the United States, we ought to take a look at what is happening elsewhere. All over Latin America there have sprung up hundreds of *comunidades de base* (basic ecclesial communities) meeting in homes. This phenomenon embraces both Protestants and Roman Catholics.

Rosario, Argentina, for instance, has been called "a flash point of growth" in the world today. A Protestant evangelistic crusade a few years ago led to the formation of many new congregations in homes. Christian workers have recently discovered that within a 100-mile radius of Rosario (Argentina's second largest city) there are 109 towns and villages without an evangelical church. House churches already have been started in a number of those places, and there will be at least 20 new ones by the end of 1984.[1]

Also here in the United States a home is often the best place to begin a new church. This kind of congregation is defined by experts as a "solo house church":

This is the house church which stands alone as a church without
connection to a larger body. It may have denominational
affiliation and accountability, or it may be disconnected or
underground. Its small size leads to financial limitations which
restrict the availability of pastoral leadership.[2]

The key phrase in this definition is "small size." There is
no reason, however, for a church that begins like this to be
content to fill the home with 30 or 40 people and then stop.
On the contrary, the kind of church I am talking about
believes in growth, chooses to grow and does grow. If the
congregation, as it moves to bigger facilities, reaches a
Sunday morning attendance of 350 to 400, it may be time
to think of starting another congregation. But that is
another decision for another time.

To place an arbitrary limit on the size of the gathered
community by not providing room for growth is bound to
defeat the whole purpose of organizing. There is no reason
why a traditional congregation that is trying to fulfill its
evangelistic responsibilities cannot grow, even though it
does not house itself in a traditional building. Freed from
the crushing burden of a building, it probably will grow
faster.

It is common for a traditional new church development
to begin to meet in temporary headquarters for a year or
two or even more. Although the land has often been
purchased well in advance, people have to be gathered,
plans drawn, funds raised and contracts let. But since the
initial meeting place is only temporary, which fact is well
publicized, the atmosphere that develops is quite different
from that of a congregation that has avowed from the
outset its plan *not* to build.

The thrust of this book is simply to suggest that the
heretofore "temporary" be considered "permanent" from
the beginning. If the congregation, from the moment of its

inception, renounces the idea of going into a building program, then growth will take place in new dimensions.

This radical change in approach goes against the grain of normal main line policy. Let me quote from the manual of the Presbyterian Church:

Care should be taken to secure a temporary facility that is attractive and functional. It should be noted, however, that unless there are compelling reasons to the contrary, temporary facilities should be just that. The congregation should be encouraged to look forward to and plan towards a permanent facility when programmatic maturity has been reached.[3]

I would like to emphasize that there *are* "compelling reasons to the contrary." But we go on and on with the goal of "the building" as the prime objective of new church development. Let me quote part of a newspaper advertisement:

New Congregational Church in - - -. The First United Church of Christ, Congregational, will hold its grand opening service on Sunday at 10:30 AM on the top floor of the Hilton Hotel. Everyone is invited to join in the celebration of this brand new church with a magnificent ocean view. . . . This newest congregation seeks to grow to 500 members by 1985. It plans to build a beautiful building in five years, create a vital church school, develop an outstanding music program and become a major positive force in the county.[4]

Now all this may well happen, but it represents another lost opportunity. You cannot help but think what a different trajectory this new church would have if it decided not to build a building, but to stay on the top floor of the Hilton with the ocean view until or unless it outgrew that space, at which time it could look for another rented Sunday morning facility. Wouldn't that kind of announcement say volumes to the public about the approach of the Christian church to the needs of our time?

What image does the published announcement convey?

Clearly, an easy way for change to take place is for the appropriate denominational committees to become convinced to try starting churches without walls. This will require finding a new church development pastor who believes this will work and can convince the people who are being enlisted for the new church. The instances where a genuine attempt has been made to start a traditional congregation without a building in prospect are unfortunately few.

Let us assume that in a given situation all parties concerned are in agreement to start a church without walls. What is the next step? Once a small number of people have agreed to come together for worship, they should look for a place to meet. It does not need to be an "ideal" place since congregations can always move elsewhere, and after a few months of normal growth, hopefully there will be a need to move to another, larger location.

Here the experience gained in new church development with temporary quarters is most valuable. There is a long list of ingenious solutions that new church development projects have successfully employed over the years. The Presbyterian manual says, "Enquiries may be made of public school systems, shopping centers, community buildings, civic and fraternal organization and other churches." The possibilities are limitless. For generations in east central Pennsylvania and elsewhere the "house Amish" have met in barns and other outbuildings.[5]

One of the most obvious places to begin, if the denomination has been able to purchase or rent a home for the pastor, is in that house. If the home is in the area of the new church development, by far the most desirable arrangement, services can be held there initially. The objection may be raised that the minister's privacy ought not to be invaded in this way. The Presbyterian manual reads: "Do not attempt to make the pastor's residence a focus of the congregation's activity. This is unfair and dehumanizing to the pastor's family and places an unreasonable burden on them."[6] But for this kind of new church development you need a pastor and spouse who are joyously willing to assume this burden.

In a home, whether it is the minister's or someone else's, you can get anywhere from 20 to 40 people in the living/dining area, with a spillover to the kitchen, halls and stairway if necesssary. Or a two car garage can be fixed up to accommodate a like number of people. If a home is the first worship location of the new congregation, it may suffice for only a few weeks because of growth, but it is a very exciting time. A congregation gathered in a home has a New Testament flavor.

A school is an ideal place to begin a church. There are schools everywhere, and schools are seldom used on Sunday mornings. The growing congregation can progress from a single classroom to a double classroom to an auditorium or gymnasium. To be sure, in some states of the Union there are church-state complications that make it difficult to use public schools, but this can usually be resolved.

The weekly rental is apt to be nominal, but in any event it is so much less than the cost to erect and maintain a building that rent is scarcely a factor. Renting is surprisingly economical, compared to owning and maintaining a building. It is not like the difference between renting or buying a home. Whether you rent or buy, you live in a house all the time. When you rent a space to hold a Sunday morning worship service, you are only using it for one morning each week, and that modest amount of time is reflected in the cost. That is why it is astronomically more expensive to build and maintain your own church building.

Of course, the possibilities of usable rooms range far beyond a school building. It is surprising how many places there are in a typical community that are not used for anything on a Sunday morning. Not all of them, of course, are suitable, but when ingenuity and imagination come into play many of them could be used for worship.

One popular place is the upstairs meeting room at a volunteer fire hall. There are folding chairs and rest rooms, along with heat and light—in a word, the basic necessities. There are all kinds of businesses, closed on Sunday, with facilities that can be used for a gathering. Government buildings, such as courthouses and city halls, are good possibilities. Some restaurants are not open on Sunday mornings and can house congregations.

One of the best facilities in a city is a hotel (or motel). Hotels have to be open at all times, and someone is always there. They are easy to find, and there is parking. Hotels have all kinds of rooms because they are used to having various sorts of meetings.

Another possibility for a new church development is to use the facilities of another church. This has become a common practice among ethnic congregations not only in the United States but in other countries as well.[7]

Recently Methodists in Derby, England needed to find a new building but were not convinced that they should build. They approached the local Anglican parish and its vicar, Martin Leigh, who went on to steer a church-sharing arrangement through eleven councils and committees until approvals were secured. Leigh called it a great step forward in Christian unity.[8]

If the newly forming congregation is willing to meet for worship at a time other than Sunday morning at 10:30 or 11:00, it is quite likely that a congregation with a building would be delighted to make it available. This accomplishes at least three things: 1) It provides a little revenue for the host congregation to help meet its bills. 2) It makes the host congregation feel good to double the amount of time its sanctuary is used. 3) It keeps the new congregation from having to build a building.

A question occurs: If you proceed to worship in rented quarters and try to grow, won't the time come when it is very difficult to find a place big enough? Consider, however, the trend toward small congregations.[9] It may surprise you to learn that 50 percent of all the churches in America have a weekly attendance of 75 people or less, and three-fourths of all churches report fewer than 300 confirmed members. Yet pastors are embarrassed because they say, "We only have 100, we only have 200 . . . in worship." Actually, 85 percent of America's churches are at the level of 200 worshipers or less. And only two percent of all churches have over 600 in attendance. This means that the problem of finding a place to worship on Sunday morning is not as difficult as it may first appear.[10]

A word of caution: meeting in homes for worship obviously does not solve all our problems. We can fail to worship God properly even in cathedrals. It does not automatically follow that we will worship in truth if we abandon traditional church buildings for churches without walls. This is a form of theological naivete.

The place is secondary to how it is used by those gathered for worship. And because buildings are secondary, genuine worship can take place wherever two or three are gathered in spirit and in truth.[11]

Notes

1. *Global Church Bulletin,* May/June, July/August 1984, Vol. XXI, Nos. 3 & 4, Milpitas, CA, pp. 365-366.

2. Olsen's *The Base Church* describes seven different models of house church, pp. 73-78.

3. *New Church Development and Church Redevelopment,* Manual for Presbyterians, UPCUSA and PCUS, 1980.

4. Palm Beach *Post,* March 5, 1983.

5. *Philadelphia Inquirer,* June 26, 1983.

6. *Presbyterian manual,* p. 62.

7. See Chapter 11 for more thoughts on ethnic congregations.

8. *The Christian Century,* November 3, 1983, p. 1098.

9. Conclusion reached by a study cosponsored by the National Council of Churches, A.M.E. Zion Church, the Southern Baptist Convention's Sunday School Board, Lutheran Council in the USA, and

Glenmary Research Center. See *Christianity Today,* October 22, 1982, p. 64.

10. Lyle E. Schaller, *The Multiple Staff and the Larger Church,* Abington, Nashville, TN, 1980, p. 9.

11. Kenneth Ballard, "Worship: Temple or Tent?" *Theology Today,* Vol. XLI, No. 1, April 1984, pp. 82-84.

Meetings In Homes
And Elsewhere

8

At one weekend gathering held by the Community Church of Madrid in a Roman Catholic retreat center in Ciudad Ducal—about 90 mintues' drive from Madrid—we experienced a most helpful worship service. Bob Davis, then presiding officer of the church council, insisted that we should all get up early Sunday morning before breakfast and hold a worship service down by the lake, a lovely spot with grassy banks and trees. We followed Bob's suggestion, and our time together by the lake proved an unforgettable experience. We read the stories of Jesus' ministry at the lakeside and we shared our faith in a memorable way. The setting was perfect for worship there in nature's cathedral.

Looking back over 40 years in the ministry, I can see that many of the most meaningful and inspirational Christian gatherings I have attended were held in places other than a sanctuary or the rooms of a church building. Who among us can easily forget our first service around a camp fire? Or our first outdoor Easter sunrise service? Or our first prayer meeting in a hospitable home? There are really no limits on places where Christians can gather for worship.

Once a new congregation has a suitable room to hold Sunday worship, it needs to think about other activities and where to have them. If it rents a Sunday morning space, it is not normally available at other times, nor is it apt to be the kind of location you need for smaller meetings.

One of the best and most obvious places to turn is the home. Holding church meetings of various kinds in homes is certainly no novelty. But when you have a building, you feel you ought to use it. As a result, many meetings that could be held in homes almost automatically go to the church. When there is no building, it is almost a necessity for meetings to be held in homes. This is a good thing. The early Christians, we remember, met in one another's homes for the study of the Scriptures and for prayer, fellowship and sharing meals.[1]

There are many good reasons to hold meetings in homes. The atmosphere of a home is often more conducive to the affairs of the Kingdom than a bare Sunday school classroom at the church. People are genuinely pleased to offer their homes for meetings. Hospitality is one of the ancient and enduring Christian virtues.

Many people feel inhibited about speaking in public, teaching, or leading worship. But they are hospitable and appreciate the chance to practice this Christian grace. And the example becomes contagious. Over a period of a dozen years in the Community Church of Madrid, we held meetings in scores of homes, from humble to palatial. The experience was invariably a blessing to both hosts and guests.

When you have a meeting involving only a few people, you can meet in a small home or apartment. When you need space for more people, it is easy to ask someone with larger quarters to host the gathering. During milder seasons of the year it is usually possible to find someone in the congregation with a porch, patio or yard—pleasant places to meet. It goes almost without saying that meeting in homes makes it easy to serve refreshments and to break bread together.

What kinds of meetings can be held in homes? There is really no limit. One of the most useful types of meeting can be a Sunday school class. While the Community Church of Madrid was meeting in a hotel, we could usually find unused areas in other convention rooms, lobbies or elsewhere for our Sunday school classes. But on those days when there was a great deal of activity at the hotel, so rooms would be in short supply, we simply asked people living near the hotel for hospitality for Sunday school. This worked out very well.

Some have suggested that the best way to save on the high cost of educational facilities is not to build them at all, to cut out Sunday school and have children taught at home. One pastor writes: "Rooms for worship are more essential to Christian churches than Sunday school facilities, and a wise use of money might well be to beef up staff and equipment and to stop raising little-used educational facilities."[2] This would be too radical a solution for most.

Often it is feasible to have choir practice in a home. Choir members sometimes have pianos or even small electronic organs. Of course committee meetings of all kinds can be held in homes. In addition, the need to seek a place for each meeting has the salutary effect of making you ask whether this meeting is really necessary. The late Paul Calvin Payne, the distinguished Presbyterian educator, was wont to say to young pastors, "Never have a meeting unless you have something to meet about."

In the experience of many, the best kind of meeting to have in a home is a meeting for Bible study and prayer. Countless congregations have discovered the efficacy of small groups like this. This is an encouraging and continuing trend in the church at large.

What about activities other than meetings? When our Madrid congregation needed a place to have a wedding, a funeral, a weekend retreat, a special evening or a holiday service, we found that we were welcomed by other Christian groups. We held weddings in Catholic chapels and in all kinds of Protestant churches. Pastors and priests were invariably pleased to be asked for the use of their facilities.

As we all know from experiences in stewardship, giving does something special for the giver, who has a need to give. Established congregations with buildings find that it is most helpful to them to share their facilities with purposely buildingless congregations. You do not need to worry about not having a building of your own. Whatever the occasion, you will find Christians with buildings who are happy to share them.

If you decide not to have a building you also will need to find places for all-day and weekend meetings. Here again the Madrid congregation was welcomed by various retreat and conference centers, especially Catholic ones who were invariably pleased that we had asked for the use of their centers.

It is common for congregations with buildings to go to other places for retreats, but if you have no real estate of your own to begin with, you are impelled to seek places for such gatherings. Often when we would express our thanks to another group for the use of their grounds and buildings for meetings like this, the reply would come: "Don't thank us. You have done more for us than we have done for you."

Far from hindering or crippling your congregation, the lack of a building of your own frees you to try new things, to search out ideal places that you can rent or borrow. At the same time you can avoid the routine and monotony into which it is so easy to fall when you use the same building for everything. Are we not called to be a pilgrim people?[3]

Liberated from the burden of maintaining a church structure, church members are much freer to become involved in social problems and are more available to serve "the lowest, the loneliest and the lost." To do this effectively, you really don't need to "meet" anywhere, but you do need to be available to go boldly "into the world" where the problems exist, and where the power of the Spirit is tremendously needed.

Contemplating the buildingless church helps us in our understanding of the church as people. Years ago this illustration appeared in a communicants' class manual: Suppose you are walking down the street and someone stops to ask you where St. Paul's Lutheran Church is. Your natural tendency is to reply: "Go to the next corner, turn right, go one block and you will see the church at the corner of State and Main." Is not the better answer to this question: "Well, at this hour, some of them are at work, some are in school, a number are at home, a few are in the hospital, others are traveling," and so on?

Functioning effectively as a gathered, beloved community of God's children, without depending on your own walls, without even a place to call your own, can be a lively and fruitful adventure in the Spirit.

Notes

1. Acts 2:46.
2. Letter in *The Christian Century*, December 10, 1980, p. 1228, written by Rev. John Holte Hagen, ALC.
3. Hebrews 11:13.

What Kind Of
Congregation Develops?

9

Did you ever wish you could ask your minister about something he or she is saying in the sermon? This has been a time-honored practice in some parts of the church, and we found it to be invaluable in the Community Church.

Any congregation, but especially a buildingless congregation, can develop in new directions concerning its attitudes toward preaching. Something interesting in this regard happened to the Community Church of Madrid. The small group of people who began the congregation advanced a helpful thought about preaching long before we started to hold services. They suggested that it would be appropriate to give the congregation more participation in the sermon. So we decided to try this approach right from the very first service of worship.

The method chosen is extraordinarily simple. Immediately at the close of the sermon, with no hymn intervening, the minister might say: "What would you like to ask me about what I have said this morning? Or would you care to offer any of your own observations about the passage of Scripture we have been talking about? Feel free to agree or disagree." And so the dialogue begins.

I have to admit that after many years of conventional preaching, I was startled by the immediate and wholehearted acceptance of what we came to call dialogue preaching.[1] I knew, intellectually, that the people in the pews were reading and studying Scripture, praying and grappling with the issues of daily Christian living just as I was, but I was touched, moved and humbled to sense the depth of wisdom, piety and Christian experience of those present. The time of dialogue became a great time of learning and sharing not only for the congregants but for the pastor, as we shared insights about the Bible and the Christian life.

To preach while anticipating an immediate verbal reaction from the congregation is a challenging and delightful experience. This is the way preaching has been from time to time in the history of the church. One scholar has found that in the 17th and 18th centuries in America, lay participation in questioning the biblical exegesis and theology of the sermon was both "normative and welcome." [2] A recent visitor to a Catholic church in Cuernavaca, Mexico tells of witnessing priests during homilies calling for—and receiving—opinions from lay people in the congregation.[3]

Doing this changes your preaching style and alters the rules of homiletics you learned in seminary. It forces you to be terse, concise and humble. Sometimes you have to say, "I'm sorry, I don't know the answer to that question." Early on I learned to ask for someone to volunteer an answer to whatever question I could not answer. Usually there was a more than adequate reply.

I also learned to reduce my sermons to about twelve to 14 minutes, which would leave about 20 minutes for the dialogue, and we managed to fit the entire worship service into 70 minutes or so. This kind of preaching became the chief characteristic of the Community Church of Madrid, along with its no building stance. I can't help but feel that the nontraditional setting helped bring about a nontraditional (but tremendously satisfying) approach to preaching.

The German theologian Jurgen Moltmann makes an interesting comment about this:

Our state churches know only the charisma of the preacher [who] is hired specifically as the one with the charisma, the one who has the Spirit. The others should listen to what [this one] says and believe what [this one] preaches. I find this attitude to be extremely narrow. The New Testament pictures the body of Christ as composed of many members, but in our state churches the body of Christ consists of one big mouth and many little ears.[4]

It is hard to convey the kind of feeling that invariably grips the congregation as the dialogue begins. The threshold of attention is palpably raised. Lay people are very much interested to hear what other lay people have to say on spiritual themes, and we clergy so seldom give them this chance! There was sometimes a brief wait for the first question, but once the ice was broken the questions and comments always came thick and fast.

Can you imagine standing before a congregation week after week and saying, "Please, only one or two more comments, because it is time to sing the final hymn and pronounce the benediction." To this day in the Community Church of Madrid, people do not seem to want the service to stop.

It is also a joy to have people leave church without the usual mumbled and perfunctory: "That was a fine sermon." Instead, the comments at the door invariably centered on what was said in the dialogue, or perhaps what that individual didn't take the opportunity to say.

When we began, we thought that once the congregation reached 50 or so it might be difficult to continue the dialogue after the sermon, but it was not. The attendance climbed to 100, then 150, then 200—and the dialogue continued, because the people wanted it.

Some of our best dialogue took place on special days when the attendance went up to 250 or 300. There may be a point at which there are too many worshipers present to have a good dialogue, but most congregations are not likely to reach it. And any congregation would profit from dialogue after the sermon, no matter how many or how few worshipers are in attendance.

Some words of caution: if you start this way in a new congregation, be prepared to continue, because people like it so much they do not want to give it up. We were often amused to have people say, on returning to the Community Church after an absence, "I could hardly wait to get back to our church where I can always get up and ask the minister about the sermon."

Over the years in Madrid, many pastors who worshiped with us were so taken with our dialogue style of preaching that they went home and tried it in their own churches. According to a number of reports received, it seldom worked or at least it did not fulfill the expectations of the preacher.

After thinking about this we decided that to have this method function easily you should start the church this way from the beginning. Otherwise, in an ongoing congregation, you are faced with the need for very careful preparation for its introduction. Once a congregation has become accustomed to the traditional style of preaching, where the worshiper is not invited to respond verbally, it may be impractical to invoke a more demanding approach.

In the dialogue situation, even if a given worshiper does not ask a question or make a comment, the atmosphere of a common search for truth via dialogue compels each one to listen and to participate emotionally and spiritually, if not verbally. Traditional churchgoers, who are accustomed to being preached *to*, are not usually going to want to change unless they go to a congregation with a different tradition already established.

As I look back over my own preaching ministry, I regret that only the last third was involved with dialogue. When you are anticipating the immediate and direct participation of the congregation in the sermon, you can hardly wait for Sunday to arrive. One of our members once said: "In our church the minister begins the sermon, but the congregation finishes it."

This kind of shared homiletic venture, with so many built-in practical and spiritual advantages, is easy to undertake in a new congregation, especially a congregation without a building of its own, because the nontraditional setting may just make possible this exhilarating experience. The sermon time is never dull when everybody has a chance to be in it.

One of the joys of working with a church without walls is to see the kind of congregation that develops. Most congregations have a tremendous loyalty to their buildings, and their pastor shares this feeling, which is natural. But when the congregation does not own real estate and uses rented or borrowed facilities, that kind of loyalty is not created. In its place there emerges a very deep sense of the church as people and strong person-to-person loyalties develop.

This is not to say that a traditional congregation with buildings cannot have this same kind of loyalty. People-centeredness is easier to achieve, however, when there are only people involved and when there is not a building to siphon off a large share of their energy and concern.

Having been the pastor of both kinds of congregations, I have seen this to be true. I notice it in myself. Although I shared the love of the people for their buildings when I was involved in standard congregations, I became aware of a new dimension in my relationships when none of my own time and energy had to be devoted to a building. The church is people (theologically, the body of Christ), and I think it is easier to develop this New Testament sense of the church as "the beloved community" when you do not have to be so completely and thoroughly engrossed in the congregation's housing.

I didn't anticipate this reaction when the Community Church of Madrid began; it is something that quietly happened along the way. And the fact that this buildingless congregation was such a joyful and liberating experience has led me to want to share this with other Christians. I might add that scores of people involved in the Community Church of Madrid over the years have responded much as I did and have urged me to tell the story publicly as I am doing here.

This overseas congregation attracted many visitors because of its no building stance. Many people who came to us were returning to the church from a dropout status. Often they admitted to having fallen away because they became tired of contributing to building funds and because they were disturbed to see so much money assigned to new organs, new carpets, new stained glass windows, heating bills and roof or furnace repairs.

Often these were people highly sensitive to the social demands of the gospel, who were looking for a way to relate themselves more directly to those in need and who wanted to give their time, talents and money to helping the poor—with whom Jesus so freely and frequently identified himself. I believe that the Community Church of Madrid would not have attracted these dropouts if we had had a traditional, building-bound program.

Of course a traditional congregation with a building can reach out effectively to the suffering and the poor. But a building is a given that, whether we like it or not, establishes certain priorities that must be met before we can reach out to others. The problem in our time is that our thousands upon thousands of buildings all too often act as barriers to the congregation's desires to break through to those who are so desperately in need of ministry.

We very much need to have more new church developments that decide never to build. If this does happen, more and more time, talent and money will be free to flow toward the amelioration of the lot of the poor who, as the Scriptures say, are always with us.[5]

The kind of congregation that develops in a church without walls also tends to be generous, because it is so easy to see where the money goes. The church council was able to say to the congregation of the Community Church of Madrid: "We will give away all monies over and above what is needed for the pastor's salary and for the modest contributions we give for the use of our Sunday morning facilities." The people were challenged by this situation and they could see how a significant portion of their giving was immediately available for needy persons and causes.

So much did this prove to be the case that from the beginning we were able to dispense with the usual stewardship paraphernalia we were all accustomed to. We decided, since we were not going to build any building, that we could do away with stewardship campaigns, pledges and offering envelopes. Nor did we have (or seek) any endowment funds.

We stated in straightforward fashion that we would do nothing to raise funds except to pass the offering plate on Sunday mornings, and we never did more than that. We said, "Your giving is a reflection of your commitment to Jesus Christ, and we will endeavor to help you with that commitment. The more committed we all are, the more money we will find in the offering."

It will take very little imagination to sense what a relief it would be to do away with the "Every Member Canvass" and all that goes with it. We only had two figures in the Madrid budget: the salary of the pastor and the cost of acquiring our room for Sunday worship. And this arrangement worked. Over a period of a dozen years we always contributed much more than enough to cover the budget so we gave away everything else as we went along. No balances were retained in the treasury at year's end.

Other churches have also found this to be true. For

instance, Charles Olsen, speaking of a buildingless congregation in Pennsylvania, writes:

Without the strain of maintaining a building and paying other overhead, their giving is channeled to ministries in the urban ghetto, to alleviating world poverty, to retreat and education centers, and to the National and World Councils of Churches.[6]

Does this not point to new directions in stewardship? Can we not trust people who have truly accepted Christ as their Lord and Savior to give what is needed, without mounting and maintaining an enormous and costly stewardship program?

Notes

1. I am aware that the sermon given by two ministers is also called dialogue preaching in some quarters.

2. Doug Adams, *Meeting House to Camp Meeting: Towards a History of American Free Church Worship from 1620 to 1834*, from a review by Harland E. Hogue in *The Christian Century*, April 27, 1983.

3. Rob Cogswell, *The Christian Century*, Dec. 14, 1983, p. 1162.

4. Miroslav Volf, "Communities of Faith and Radical Discipleship," an interview with Jurgen Moltmann in *The Christian Century*, 1983, p. 247.

5. Matthew 26:11.

6. Olsen, *The Base Church*, p. 113.

Obstacles To Overcome

10

There are many obstacles to overcome if we are going to promote the idea of churches without walls. Attending a committee meeting overseas I heard a national Christian leader say: "We have got to build an impressive building in ---, otherwise they won't pay any attention to us."

This statement was practical, perhaps, but theologically reprehensible. Do we really expect people to pay attention to us Christians simply because we have some imposing church buildings?

The economist and writer John Kenneth Galbraith suggests in *The Anatomy of Power* that

In the earliest Christian days power originated with the compelling personality of the Savior. Almost immediately an organization, the Apostles, came into being, and in time the church as an organization became the most influential . . . in the world. Not the least of its sources of power was its property and the income thus disposed.[1]

But over the centuries this has changed. Galbraith remarks, "The property of the church has declined greatly in relative importance as a source of power. Once of magnificent extent, it is now of minor magnitude when compared to secular resources."[2] We are deceiving ourselves if we think that we can help bring in the Kingdom through massive buildings. The mission of the church, at its best, has always been people-centered and not temple-centered.

There are other obstacles that prevent the idea of a church without walls from catching on.

One of the most powerful forces at work in human life is inertia. We are often not fully aware that we are creatures of habit. Most church members hate to have their routines disturbed, no matter how compelling the reasons. Even a comparatively minor change, such as a different hour for worship, calls forth a strident, "We never did it that way before."

Resistance to change, unfortunately, is a strand that runs through the entire history of the church. All too often the church catches up to, rather than leads, change in society. In fact someone once called the phrase, "We never did it that way before," the "Seven Last Words of the Church."

Imagine the scorn heaped on the suggestion to build the first Christian church building centuries ago. Surely the leading member of the congregation stood and said: "We never did it that way before."

Pastors with whom I have discussed the central idea expressed in these pages have usually shaken their heads and voiced their doubts. "People are used to having a building of their own and want to have it; I don't think people can be persuaded to change their thinking and practice," one thoughtful friend told me. "How are you going to keep people from feeling like orphans?" another asked.

It is true that the typical congregation huddles up to its building the way Linus clutches his security blanket, but it doesn't have to be that way. When church members learn to depend on each other instead of a building, they won't feel like orphans. On the contrary they will be strengthened by bonds that are much closer than those that tie so many of us emotionally to our sanctuaries.

Another obstacle is that old devil, pride—the first in the classic list of the seven deadly sins. Here I use pride in the New Testament sense, *hubris*. The Apostle Paul states unequivocally: "God forbid that I should glory, save in the cross of our Lord Jesus Christ, by whom the world is crucified unto me, and I unto the world."[3]

Ignoring the Pauline dictum, we cheerfully boast about our church buildings, and in so doing mistake the substance for the spirit. When we have a building, we tend to boast about it.

Now I am not saying it is wrong per se to be proud of your building. Church buildings, especially cathedrals, do represent devotion, sacrifice, commitment, labor and love. The urge to erect beautiful, expensive buildings is not a phenomenon unique to our generation. But too many pastors think they are falling down on the job if they are not continually involved in building ever bigger and better houses of worship, educational wings, parish halls and recreational centers.[4]

The tradition of pride in our edifices can easily become a substitute for the gospel message itself, even pride in the glory that belongs uniquely to God. It is so much easier to be proud of the building than it is to be proud of something less tangible. Also, pride in the church structure and its annexes can easily become overweening pride.

I know this from personal experience. As pastor in one town, I was proud of our gymnasium, especially since none of the other churches in that town had a gymnasium. I was proud of our new pipe organ, especially because it produced a tone so brilliant that the organ company brought prospective customers from the whole area to hear it. I was extraordinarily proud of our beautiful new stained glass windows, because I had picked the themes and helped determine the content.

When we have a congregation without a building, neither the pastor nor the members will be able to brag about it. This may not be a valid reason to avoid building a sanctuary, but it is surely a positive consequence of not having one. Perhaps the only time pride in our buildings is legitimate is when it takes a distant second to our pride in the gospel.

It is time to single out the person who is often the villain in the piece, and that is the parson. It has been well said that many ministers suffer from an edifice complex. We try to convince ourselves that we would like to be remembered for our faithfulness to the gospel, for those who have been led to Christ through our ministry, for those to whom we have ministered in the joys and sorrows of life, and especially for those who have "entered the ministry" from churches we serve.

But the easiest thing of all to be remembered for is our edifice, that is, the church we built or the --- we built when we were the pastor in ---. Human nature makes it virtually impossible not to brag about your building.

The Scripture says, "Blessed are the dead who die in the Lord . . . for their deeds follow them."[5] But when we think of being remembered by posterity, we cannot help but point with pride to what has been constructed, building-wise, under our pastoral aegis.

Before we criticize Robert Schuller and the Crystal Cathedral, we should be aware that a host of pastors share his desire. What may upset us most is that he actually built his, and we did not! That towering glass sanctuary in Orange County, California may be an example of an ecclesiastical edifice complex in our time, but it is surely not the only one. Jesus said in the Sermon on the Mount,

"You impostor! Take the log out of your own eye first, and then you will be able to see and take the speck out of your brother's eye."[6]

Let me give a couple of examples of what the pastor's edifice complex can lead to:

One congregation I am acquainted with had a minister nearing retirement. The congregation owned a small building, but with multiple services it was adequate. The minister, however, had a heart set on building a new church before retiring and persuaded a few special friends in the congregation to get behind the project. Just as this pastor retired, the new building was completed. Now, the successor has to pay off the mortgage. And the congregation has probably lost the opportunity to go to a growing section of the community and begin a mission, which in all probability would have quickly developed into a self-supporting congregation.

Often the idea of relocating to build new facilities is threatening and divisive. I know of a congregation that has been many years at its present site, a downtown area that has changed and is no longer primarily residential. But the town is not that large, and people can still return from the outskirts (in five or ten minutes by car) to take part in the activities of the congregation.

For a year or two the minister has been insisting that the congregation should buy a large tract outside the community and erect a whole new set of buildings—a campus. Some people in the congregation believe that it would be a sinful waste of money to relocate and rebuild when the present situation is quite viable. They are concerned, and perhaps they are right, that their pastor is moved primarily by a desire to "make a name" in the proposed rebuilding. Already some people have left the church in protest over what they see as a forthcoming ecclesiastical boondoggle.

Suppose this congregation were a church without a building, renting a space adequate for Sunday morning worship. If the need for relocation were definitely established and agreed upon, how easy and how inexpensive it would be to find a new space to rent on Sunday mornings out in the new neighborhood.

Donald R. Allen writes about the experience of Trinity Presbyterian Church in Harrisonburg, Virginia. The Presbytery had been given a four and one-half acre property that included a large antebellum house. The First Presbyterian Church of Harrisonburg voted in 1962 *not* to move out to the new property. So Allen became the organizing minister of a new congregation at the site rejected by the downtown church.

Predictions of rapid growth and a future edifice were proudly voiced by church authorities, but the people made an important decision: to renovate the house instead of razing it to make way for building a church. The congregation was released from immediate pressure to build, and the decision eventually was made not to build a regular church edifice. The pastor reports that the tendency to emphasize a physical plant was "not easily overcome, nor is it ever buried permanently." He says that on the occasions when they anticipate a congregation too big for the old house, they simply rent a school auditorium, or go outdoors.[7]

The pastor's edifice complex, which is usually seconded by many lay people, may not be considered a sin. But I wonder if building new churches in our time does not represent, in all too many cases, sin in the sense of *hamartia,* missing the mark.

Charles Olsen writes:

The church's utter dependence on a place reveals an adolescent behavior pattern. When the church comes to a mature understanding of the gospel, valuing life together and mission to the world, it can be weaned from this dependency. Then the edifice complex will no longer rob the church of its vital energy and resources.[8]

A congregation can gain a lot when it decides to gather for worship in a place that is used for something else six days a week. Perhaps our sin is two-fold: our failure to understand that this can be done, and our failure to try to do it. If we want to be faithful stewards of God's bounty, can we not find needier and more worthy causes than the erection of new church buildings? ˙

Notes

1. John Kenneth Galbraith, *The Anatomy of Power*, Houghton-Mifflin, Boston, 1983, p. 7.

2. Ibid, p. 172.

3. Galatians 6:14, KJV.

4. Bruce Larson and Ralph Osborne, *The Emerging Church*, Word Books, Waco, TX, 1970, p. 23.

5. Revelation 14:13.

6. Matthew 7:5, TEV.

7. Allen, *Barefoot in the Church*, p. 141.

8. Olsen, *The Base Church*, p. 145.

Churches Without Walls
And Church Growth

11

Have you ever had anything to do with an ethnic congregation? If you have, you know that these groups of believers are often small, and so have trouble raising funds for buildings and other purposes. Although they are usually welcome to meet at off-hours in existing church buildings, it is a problem for them to build their own facilities. This has slowed the planting of ethnic congregations, despite the great need that exists for them in polyglot America.

Denominations are taking measures to help. In 1984 the Presbyterian Church USA agreed to provide funding for 13 new projects: 3 Hispanic; 3 Native American; 2 Formosan; 2 Korean; 1 Chinese; 1 Filipino; 1 Vietnamese.[1]

Also, a National Convocation on Evangelizing Ethnic America has been called to meet in Houston in April 1985, with the theme "Let Ethnic America Hear His Voice." A willingness to create churches without walls would greatly accelerate our response to this need.

The entire subject of church growth, not only for ethnic groups but for everybody, is crucial for our times. Whether we reach 2000 A.D. with the same, a greater or a lesser proportion of the world's population in the Christian fold obviously depends on the rate of church growth.

In the United States the growth rate of church membership has fallen behind that of the general population, which reverses a trend. Between 1952 and 1971 churches were growing more rapidly than the population, with a growth rate of 46 percent, compared with a 35 percent rate in the population. Between 1971 and 1980, however, population growth increased at a rate of 11.5 percent, while church membership grew by only 4.1 percent.[2]

If denominational decision makers in the United States can be persuaded to try seriously to develop new congregations without buildings, we could look for a tripling, at the very least, in their number. The New Testament way and the only known way of increasing the number of believers is to set about gathering them into congregations for subsequent discipling, so the rate at which new congregations are to be established is crucial.

All Christians would agree to the need for accelerating this rate of growth. Let us start new congregations that are liberated at the very beginning from the burden of the "first unit" (and all that follows). Here is a sound procedure for real church growth.

The amount of money saved by starting buildingless congregations would be considerable. Just in 1982, for instance, the United Presbyterian Church approved loans for church building aid in the amount of $4,726,318. These funds helped purchase 21 sites and 12 manses and built or rehabilitated 41 church units. Of this number, 34 were new church developments, which received a total of $2,867,980.[3]

For some time, we have had a surplus of clergy in the main line denominations. We are told there are not enough congregations to go around.

Let us start more new congregations! Many capable

pastors are available to do this work. Perhaps questions need to be asked about how the church is training pastors for new church development. And how are part-time pastors being used in tent-making ministries? The sticking point remains not the supply of pastors, but rather the enormous financing needed to plan, build, monitor and maintain a building.

It should be noted that our brothers and sisters in Christ who live in the Third World are ahead of us in this regard. Traditional structures are still being built in Africa, Asia and Latin America, but more and more congregations are starting and staying in homes, storefronts or some other location that is not a traditional structure. Use of indigenous architecture, when there is a structure, has brought costs way down and has enabled many congregations to have a simple place to meet.

The explosion in the number of Third World believers that David Barrett, an Anglican priest and research scholar, and his colleagues have written about has given abundant proof of the inexhaustible vitality and self-propagating nature of the Christian faith.[4]

Rev. Jerry Porter, a missionary of the Church of the Nazarene, reports how students were key workers in launching scores of new churches in Costa Rica:

A lot of people have said, "Well, I don't have the gift of starting a new church. I can't do it." These . . . are pastors who have never done it, and they are scared. We are trying to get that fear out of them before they leave school. They have done it, and we don't invest a lot of money in these experiments. We are not paying rent for a building, we are not paying salary for a pastor . . . we are just totally following the Lord's leading. If it grows, the group pays a little bit of rent. If it fizzles, we have not lost any investment. We have not built some big building.[5]

Rev. John Mizuki, pastor of the Japanese division of the Mission Valley Free Methodist Church in San Gabriel, California feels there is a need for 500 new churches just for evangelism among the Japanese. He says, however:

> When I suggest the planting of 500 new churches, I am not
> thinking of the conventional type of churches with costly edifices
> and salaried pastors. I am rather thinking of the New Testament
> type of house churches with unpaid or half-paid pastors which
> may be established with little cost. To plant many small churches
> that would be led by lay ministers seems to be the answer to the
> pressing task of Christianizing the Japanese in this country.[6]

The Missionary Church in northern Sierra Leone says
that many new churches are being planted, and that the
new congregations gather in homes purchased for the
purpose, in community centers, schools, study centers,
homes for the elderly and apartments.[7]

Sometimes our Western mission boards seem to
condition and reduce church growth possibilities in the
undeveloped countries by taking for granted that
congregations cannot be started until the financing of a
certain kind of structure is guaranteed. Yet we know from
the beginning that this edifice will be expensive and
difficult to maintain and have quite limited use in terms of
hours per week.

In the race to win the minds and hearts of people for
Christ, as we strive to obey the Great Commission,
Christians in the United States have been outdistanced by
believers in the Third World. Year by year we are
becoming more mired down by our unthinking insistence
on following tradition in regard to structures to house our
gathered communities. Are we so silly, are we so obdurate,
are we so shortsighted, that we will persevere in this stance,
come what may?

Richard Foster, a university professor who has thought
philosophically about these issues, writes:

> In the final analysis, our decisions about architecture and
> buildings will be determined by our theology of the church. . . .
> Any attempt to deal with simplicity in the church cannot avoid

the use of buildings and architecture. . . . This is not an issue that yields an easy answer.[8]

A number of congregations which take their mission seriously have decided deliberately to give away to missions and benevolence an amount equal to the amount they spend on new buildings. This is not easy, and not many congregations attempt it. Even fewer succeed.

There is a large main line charismatic congregation in Virginia that has been able to do this. The insight behind this practice is commendable and surely the poor are helped tremendously. But the net result is still a building to maintain.

The building committee at the Tabernacle Church of Christ in Columbus, Indiana asked itself, "Why is a monumental building desirable to the practice of Christianity, the humblest of faiths?" Here is how it answered the question:

> A costly church can be justified, in our opinion, only so far as it inspires and stimulates people in living better lives. . . . People do make Christians of other people and people do help each other to accomplish Christian ends. . . . We are all very sensitive to our surroundings. . . .
>
> Great buildings dominate and influence the lives of all who live near them. A church which embodies and illustrates the truths of Christianity should be a monument in which the affection and aspiration of many generations of Christians are centered. That is why we chose to spend our money in this way. We want our labor, in the form of this building, to continue to influence the lives of our children and of theirs, to remind those who pass of Christ and to renew his spirit among us.[9]

Although it is encouraging to have the question asked, I see few instances of new congregations eschewing the goal of their own building. So we are apparently condemned to repeat the cycle that has left the United States covered with underused, horribly expensive and, often, eventually ill-located structures for worship.

Professor Sam Moffett of Princeton Seminary has a thought that I find appropriate here: "The church that is turned in upon itself has turned its back on the world to which it was sent by Jesus Christ."[10]

Notes

1. *Monday Morning,* February 6, 1984, p. 32.

2. Reported in *The Christian Century,* Dec. 22-29, 1982, p. 1300.

3. Reported in *Monday Morning* magazine, January 17, 1983, p. 34.

4. David B. Barrett, Editor, *The World Christian Encyclopedia,* Oxford University Press, 1982, passim.

5. *Global Church Growth Bulletin,* Santa Clara, CA, Nov.-Dec. 1982, p. 225.

6. Ibid, p. 228.

7. Ibid, p. 232.

8. Richard J. Foster, *Freedom of Simplicity,* Harper & Row, San Francisco, 1981, pp. 152-153.

9. *A.D.,* July-August 1983, p. 13.

10. Sam Moffett, "The Greatest Enemy Is Within," in *The Church in New Frontiers,* MARC, Monrovia, CA, 1983.

From Steeple
To People

12

Imagination is paramount in any Christian enterprise. Some years ago there was a Methodist congregation in Buenos Aires that felt a newer and bigger building was necessary for its continued growth, so it sold its old building to an Armenian evangelical congregation.

Within a few months, with great imagination and a relatively modest expenditure of funds, the Armenians transformed that old building into a beautiful and highly useful church. Meanwhile, the other group went on for years in temporary quarters, waiting for funds from the United States to build its dream church.

I do not want to suggest the abandonment of existing church buildings, nor to recommend tearing them down. I would suggest, however, that if you already have a building, you think long and hard before you build another one. Many times it is easier and less expensive to fix up the building you have. To do this is often better than erecting new structures.

It is depressing to hear of countless congregations who decide to abandon their buildings and go out into the countryside (in the direction of anticipated population growth), proceed to blacktop 50 acres of ground, and then begin to build a campus of church buildings. Instead, look around at the possibilities of starting one or more churches without walls out there where people live.

Some might solemnly object that Christians who are used to the comfort and inspiration of their own building could not be happy in a no walls situation. Yet our experience proved that many of the people at the Community Church of Madrid who had come from typical congregations with buildings quickly adjusted to the new situation and even learned to like it better. They particularly liked the opportunity to give money to benevolences and missions rather than spending it on bricks, mortar and maintenance. Over and over these folk indicated that, though they tried, they could not find a church without walls when they moved elsewhere.

To be sure, there are always those who are put off by a major change. Once in a great while, people came to our church in Madrid and, on learning that we did not have a building or any plans to construct one, would quietly flee to the refuge of a traditional congregation.

Obviously the building of churches is not going to come to a crashing halt. Consider, however, the example of St. Paul's Episcopal Church in Darien, Connecticut. This charismatic congregation, under the leadership of Rev. Everett L. Fullam, has experienced unusually rapid growth. Hundreds crowd into their services each Sunday. The number of communicants more than quadrupled in four years. The number of Sunday services grew to four. It was clear that the church had to respond to this growth in some way.

Bob Slosser, an author interested in the story of that congregation, reports:

The climax came in the spring of 1977—a moment of threatening darkness and the smell of defeat, followed by a burst of light and the sweet fragrance of victory. The Lord first closed many distracting doors, then set St. Paul's on an altered course with a new, yet ancient, concept of the church of Jesus Christ. Things were never to be the same.[1]

What happened? The church formed a Facilities Planning Commission because of a general agreement that there was a need to build. The vote of the vestry was unanimous. The people offered prayer for guidance as to how much they should build.

The Senior Warden had a word of wisdom to build a church as large as possible on the present property and the architects went ahead with plans and drawings. But the Darien Planning and Zoning Commission unanimously rejected the plans, saying they would constitute an overextensive use of the property.

At that point the Facilities Planning Commission tried other avenues, such as looking into the purchase of additional property or merging with existing congregations with larger buildings. Nothing worked. Finally this recommendation was made to the vestry: 1) that St. Paul's commit itself to the building of the living church, not a building to house St. Paul's church, and 2) that a commitment be made to the use of public facilities.

As of this writing, St. Paul's is meeting in a high school auditorium, still using its present buildings to the fullest possible extent for Sunday school, youth and midweek meetings. What a tremendous vision there is here!

Fullam said:

We have the opportunity to demonstrate the truth of what we believe, that the church is not a building and that it doesn't even depend upon a building; that God will be where his people gather; and that we are indeed a pilgrim people called to follow him wherever he shall go.[2]

Later in the message, he addressed the problem of where to meet:

If we want to have a parish dinner, and our parish is far too large to have a dinner here in this building, then we'll rent the Holiday Inn or some other place. Or if we want more offices than we can have in this building, then we can go down to an office building in Darien or somewhere around and rent such facilities. I can tell you, even at Darien prices, rent is a pittance compared to what we would pay in interest on the mortgage we were contemplating for the building of bricks and mortar.

This recommendation to use public facilities underscores the fact that the church is not a building. St. Paul's is wherever St. Paul's people are gathering to worship the Lord and praise him. That is what we are called to do.[3]

The use of the high school is considered by the congregation to be regular and not temporary. Even though the present church is being expanded to its limit according to zoning regulations, the pastor emphasized that "this is not so we can come back, so don't entertain that hope, but we need seating capacity for our week-time ministry."[4]

I would encourage existing congregations with buildings to consider the example of St. Paul's, Darien, when growth demands some response. Make sure of your theological position before you build.

Charles Olsen, the expert on house churches whom I have frequently quoted, reminds us that, although the church is not dependent on a special place, it does need space. He does not believe that we need church buildings in the number that now exist. But people rarely picture "church" without seeing a space.

Some writers say that people need a "place" and that our buildings provide a symbolic identity and an emotional security framework, but peak religious experiences occur not only in the sanctuary but also in intimate small groupings and even in times of solitude.

Olsen also charges that we are still reaping the whirlwind of the medieval belief that God was offered through the Mass, a peak religious event that was enclosed in a church building. "I would say that people do not need a religious place so much as they need a religious experience."[5]

Ralph Osborne and Bruce Larson, although they are both Presbyterian ministers whose congregations have traditional structures, question church buildings. They say that the last three decades have marked the busiest period of construction in the history of the church.

Wherever we go we are struck by the quantity of new construction and major rebuilding projects undertaken since the close of World War II. . . . We must observe from personal experience that not much of permanent value seems to be happening within a good number of these magnificent buildings. Much too often we have sensed a "business as usual" quality to church life. If a congregation has set as its primary goal the building of a place fit for the worship of Almighty God, it will find disillusionment when the project is completed. Unless something has happened to the people, the place is not very important.[6]

Donald Allen wants us to remember that the church exists for the world and not for itself. Its own buildings and programs are secondary to its life, service and witness. He insists that to the writers of the New Testament, the church as the people of God could appear as a reality in any setting with any number of persons. Obviously the church was never seen by the first Christians as a building, be it house or temple. It was and is wherever people gather and live out their life in God's name.[7]

Barbara Woody, program assistant for congregational development in the Presbyterian Church, USA, is also concerned about buildings. She believes that much more emphasis has been given to church (building) formation than to community (people) formation. "The building is not primarily the mission of the church," she states. "Our mission is to be faithful to God. The building is only one instrument. Church development, redefined, is community formation, with buildings only vehicles to help in that process." [8]

One final consideration that weighs very heavily is this: when we look at human need, how can we justify new church buildings except under the most exceptional of circumstances? William Hudnut asks, "How do you justify more buildings for affluent American church people when half the world goes to bed hungry? Is that the church as Suffering Servant? American churches must justify more buildings to the Suffering Servant. And if they can't, they better not build." [9]

Just think of the number of Americans without a place to live: some estimates range as high as two million plus. That number is expected to increase to three million. Mary Ellen Holmes, coauthor of *Homeless in America: A Forced March to Nowhere,* recently testified before a House Subcommittee on Housing: "The homeless population is growing astronomically and changing radically." [10]

One wonders if main line churches can ever make significant inroads among the poor. The poor, when they go to church, go to storefronts and sect groups. They simply cannot afford to participate in the life of congregations with large, luxurious, costly buildings. This is a tremendous problem.

If we are sincere in our resolve to seek out all those for whom Christ died with the good news of the gospel, it behooves us to rethink our approach. Simply by the kind of buildings we normally build, we make it difficult for the poor to share in the adventure of the gospel by our way of living out the gospel. This is just one more area where there needs to be prayerful research as we move toward the 21st century. Can we have an inclusive church if we continue to build expensive sanctuaries?

I have wanted to share with other Christians the joy and freedom we found at the Community Church of Madrid simply by taking as our beginning the principle that we would not erect a building of our own. Others have done the same, and I am confident that if these examples begin to be imitated, by dozens and then scores and then hundreds of new church developments, we would greatly please God and advance the Kingdom. We might even set the stage for a return, in the 21st century, to the atmosphere of the glorious early centuries of the faith, when churches were people.

Notes

1. Bob Slosser, *Miracle in Darien*, Logos International, Plainfield, NJ, 1979, p. 253.

2. Ibid, p. 258.

3. Ibid, p. 257.

4. Ibid, pp. 258–259.

5. Olsen, *The Base Church*, pp. 144-145.

6. Ibid, p. 23

7. Allen, *Barefoot in the Church*, pp. 19, 26.

8. Barbara Woody, "From Steeple to People," *Presbyterian Survey*, June 1984, p. 33.

9. Hudnut, *Arousing the Sleeping Giant*, p. 15.

10. *The Christian Century*, March 9, 1983, p. 207.

ORDER FORM

To order an additional copy or copies of:

THE CHURCH WITHOUT WALLS

please write, or tear out this page as your handy order form.

Kindly send me _____ copies of

THE CHURCH WITHOUT WALLS

Name_____

Address_____

_____

City _____ State _____ Zip _____

I enclose $_____ with this order. *(No C.O.D.'s please)*

Each copy: $3.95, plus postage & handling $.50 total $4.45
Two copies: $8.45   Three copies: $12.45
 (Calif. residents add $.24 sales tax per copy.)

Quantity discounts:
  10-19 copies, ordered at one time: 15% discount plus
  one free copy.
  20 or more copies, ordered together: 25% discount plus
  one free copy.

fold here second

Postage

Stamp

TO: **HOPE PUBLISHING HOUSE**
        P.O. Box 60008
        Pasadena, California 91106

fold here first

ORDER FORM

To order an additional copy or copies of:

THE CHURCH WITHOUT WALLS

please write, or tear out this page as your handy order form.

Kindly send me _____ copies of

THE CHURCH WITHOUT WALLS

Name_____

Address_____

_____

City _____ State _____ Zip _____

I enclose $_____ with this order. *(No C.O.D.'s please)*

Each copy: $3.95, plus postage & handling $.50 total $4.45
Two copies: $8.45   Three copies: $12.45
(Calif. residents add $.24 sales tax per copy.)

Quantity discounts:
  10-19 copies, ordered at one time: 15% discount plus
  one free copy.
  20 or more copies, ordered together: 25% discount plus
  one free copy.

Cut or tear here

Postage

Stamp

TO: **HOPE PUBLISHING HOUSE**
P.O. Box 60008
Pasadena, California 91106

ORDER FORM

To order an additional copy or copies of:

THE CHURCH WITHOUT WALLS

please write, or tear out this page as your handy order form.

Kindly send me _____ copies of

THE CHURCH WITHOUT WALLS

Name_____

Address_____

_____

City _____ State _____ Zip _____

I enclose $_____ with this order. *(No C.O.D.'s please)*

Each copy: $3.95, plus postage & handling $.50 total $4.45
Two copies: $8.45   Three copies: $12.45
  (Calif. residents add $.24 sales tax per copy.)

Quantity discounts:
  10-19 copies, ordered at one time: 15% discount plus
    one free copy.
  20 or more copies, ordered together: 25% discount plus
    one free copy.

fold here second

Postage

Stamp

TO: **HOPE PUBLISHING HOUSE**
P.O. Box 60008
Pasadena, California 91106

fold here first

ORDER FORM

To order an additional copy or copies of:

THE CHURCH WITHOUT WALLS

please write, or tear out this page as your handy order form.

Kindly send me _____ copies of

THE CHURCH WITHOUT WALLS

Name_____

Address____ ___ _____

_____

City _____ State _____ Zip _____

I enclose $_____ with this order. *(No C.O.D.'s please)*

Each copy: $3.95, plus postage & handling $.50 total $4.45
Two copies: $8.45   Three copies: $12.45
   (Calif. residents add $.24 sales tax per copy.)

Quantity discounts:
   10-19 copies, ordered at one time: 15% discount plus
   one free copy.
   20 or more copies, ordered together: 25% discount plus
   one free copy.

Cut or tear here

fold here second

Postage

Stamp

TO: HOPE PUBLISHING HOUSE
P.O. Box 60008
Pasadena, California 91106

fold here first

Cut or tear here